Southern Living

# COMFORT
# FOOD
# *Made Easy*

## Hearty homestyle dishes for busy cooks

Oxmoor
House.

Southern Living®

# COMFORT FOOD *Made Easy*

# Contents

# Welcome

If we told you it was possible to serve your family a home-cooked meal any day of the week, you'd probably think we were crazy. With the hustle and bustle of weeknight chaos, who has time to make long, complicated recipes that make use of every pot and pan in the kitchen? In *Comfort Food Made Easy*, we've created a collection of classic homestyle recipes with quick and easy shortcuts that are low on prep time but high in flavor—so you can get dinner on the table when time is at a premium.

Before you get started, get organized with Easy Steps to Fast Meals, our user-friendly guide to the most essential kitchen ingredients and tools used throughout this book. Each chapter thereafter is organized by cooking method —such as one-dish, no cook, and slow cooker—making for easy navigation. In addition, we've rounded out our main dishes with quick but tasty sides and desserts.

We'll show you best-loved Southern classics made easy such as Jambalaya with Chicken and Sausage (page 30) in One-Dish Dinners in a Dash. In Slow-Cooked Meals to Savor, we'll introduce you to slow-cooker favorites, such as Easy Brunswick Stew (page 127). Start them in the morning and by the time you're home, dinner's ready.

In No-Cook Wonders, you'll learn how to skip the stovetop entirely—you'll be amazed at how a big batch of our Peach Gazpacho with Cucumber Yogurt (page 149) comes together in minutes! For dessert, we've created easy recipes that will wow your guests, such as Chocolate Lava Cakes (page 241) and an Apple Brown Betty (page 257).

Also here to help you are *Comfort Food Made Easy* tips straight from Southern Living Test Kitchen experts, and Simple Swaps sidebars that give flavorful variations on traditional recipes. With *Comfort Food Made Easy*, it's possible to cook a delicious, hearty meal that the entire family will love— they'll never know just how easy it was for you!

*Susan*

**Susan Ray, Editor**

# Easy Steps to Fast Meals

# Top 10 Tips
## for Quick Comfort Food

**BUY FRESH PRODUCE IN SEASON.**
Always start with fresh, peak-season ingredients,
which often need the least help and fuss in the kitchen.

**INVEST IN A GOOD BOX GRATER.**
Many comfort-food recipes—creamy grits, pimiento cheese,
cornbread—incorporate cheese. A good box-style grater will get the job done quickly.

**LET OTHERS DO THE WORK.**
Too few cooks take advantage of help at the store. Have the butcher cut, bone, or skin meat,
and ask the fishmonger to skin or fillet the fish. Buy precut fruits and vegetables, too.

**UTILIZE NO-COOK PRODUCTS.**
Explore the store for high-quality, no-cook proteins for pasta tosses, salads, or pizzas.
Jarred sustainable tuna, rotisserie chicken, smoked pork, or smoked salmon
or trout can help give you a jump-start on dinner.

**USE YOUR FREEZER WISELY.**
Label and store extra portions of sauces, sides, and entrées in the freezer. That extra cup of
pasta sauce will come in handy for pizza, meatball hoagies, or even soup.

**MAKE SURE YOU HAVE A WELL-SEASONED CAST-IRON SKILLET.**
A regional icon, this versatile pan can stand in for a sandwich press, a pizza stone, a baking dish,
or a sauté pan. From frying catfish to baking cornbread, you can do just about anything in it.

**USE YOUR MICROWAVE.**
Utilizing the microwave helps you streamline prep and cut down on the pots
and pans you have to clean later. You can quickly zap parchment-wrapped beets
for a side, soften bell peppers to stuff, or bring stock to a boil for soup.

**DO A BIT OF WORK ON THE WEEKENDS.**
On a lazy Sunday, make versatile, high-flavor components, such as roasted tomatoes,
toasted breadcrumbs, and roasted garlic, to simplify cooking later in the week.

**COOK ONCE, EAT TWICE.**
If you're planning to grill four chicken breasts, grill eight so you'll have four on hand.
When roasting vegetables, do a giant batch—it adds little time on the front end.

**INVEST IN GOOD KNIVES.**
You simplify prep greatly when you have sharp, precise knives and hone
your knife skills. Simple, quick food, often sautéed or stir-fried, needs to be
cut into uniform pieces; they're prettier, too.

# Freezer Pleasers

*Take a trip down the frozen foods aisle of the grocery store to discover some convenience products that make comfort food cooking even easier.*

**Frozen Breaded Chicken Fingers:** Get ahead of the game when it comes to quick dinners. You'll be surprised at how versatile these kid-friendly finds can be. Use them to top a pizza, on a sandwich, in a stir-fry, or on top of a salad.

**Frozen Biscuits:** They aren't just for breakfast. They can be used to create favorites such as Chicken Pot Pie (page 45), for a quick weeknight dessert (page 244), or to round out a meal.

**Frozen Vegetables:** These gems are neatly trimmed and offer consistent quality year-round. Use them in casseroles, stews (page 127), or create your own side dish by steaming them in the microwave.

**Frozen Pie Shells:** Use this store-bought, convenience product for both sweet and savory recipes. Use it to make quiches, pies, and more.

**Frozen Waffles:** Helpful for quick weeknight meals, frozen waffles can be used as sandwich "bread," as a base for chicken pot pie, as a dessert, or served on their own.

# Fridge Finds

*Keep your fridge stocked with a few of these ingredients so you can throw quick weeknight meals together in a pinch.*

**Fresh Pastas:** For those nights when you don't have the 15 minutes to cook dried fettuccine, reach for refrigerated fresh pasta. It's done in about a minute or two and is an essential ingredient in many comfort food favorites.

**Precut Produce:** You can't beat the convenience factor—some are even designed to microwave-steam in a bag. They're useful in casseroles, stir-fries, and salads.

**Bagged Lettuces:** Rinsing, drying, stemming, and chopping supermarket spinach is a messy time-eater. Ready-to-use bags of greens cut out that whole process and come in a wide assortment—spinach, mixed baby greens, romaine, and kale. And a salad is the perfect accompaniment to a one-dish meal.

**Rotisserie Chicken:** Supermarket rotisserie chicken—a moist, plump, savory bird just waiting for you to pick up and carry home—is a help to put in soups, stews, tacos, and casseroles. Stick with the original, unflavored version, as it's the most versatile.

**Large Eggs:** There's simply no protein that can be prepared as quickly as eggs, and in so many ways. Use them as a binder in patties and meatloaf or to prepare baked goods.

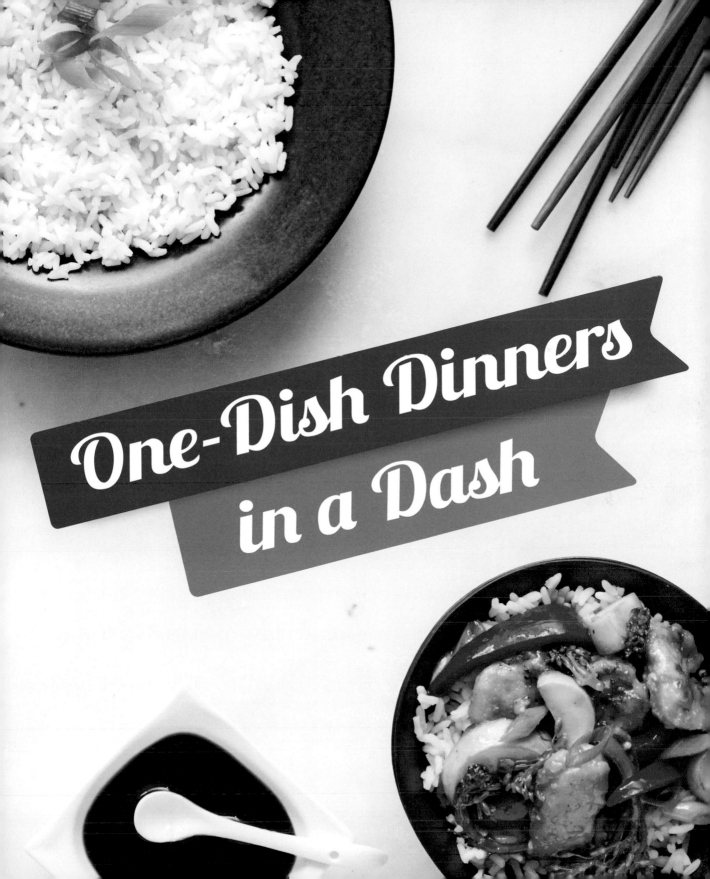

# One-Dish Dinners in a Dash

**Make It Easy:**

*Parboiling jump-starts the cooking process on the potatoes, so they get a crispy finish just about the time the steak is done.*

# Steak Kabobs

## with Fingerling Potatoes

MAKES 6 SERVINGS
HANDS-ON 45 MIN.
TOTAL 4 HOURS, 20 MIN.,
INCLUDING VINAIGRETTE

14 (8-inch) wooden or metal skewers, divided
16 small fingerling potatoes, halved
2 lb. boneless rib-eye, tri-tip, or flank steaks,
    trimmed and cut into 1 ½-inch pieces
Béarnaise Vinaigrette, divided
¼ cup butter, melted
1 cup firmly packed baby arugula
1 cup loosely packed fresh flat-leaf parsley leaves
½ cup torn fresh basil
¼ cup chopped fresh chives
¼ cup loosely packed fresh mint leaves, torn
3 Tbsp. drained capers

1. Soak 8 wooden skewers in water 30 minutes. (Omit if using metal skewers.) Meanwhile, bring potatoes and water to cover to a boil in a Dutch oven over medium-high heat; cook 10 minutes or just until crisp-tender. Drain.

2. Combine steak and ½ cup vinaigrette in a large zip-top plastic freezer bag. Thread 8 potato halves onto 1 double set of skewers (2 skewers side by side), leaving a ⅛-inch space between pieces; repeat with 3 double sets of skewers and remaining potatoes. Cut 4 to 8 crosswise slits ¼ inch deep on top of each potato. Combine potatoes and ½ cup vinaigrette in a large zip-top plastic freezer bag. Seal bags, and chill 3 hours, turning occasionally.

3. Meanwhile, soak remaining 6 wooden skewers in water 30 minutes. (Omit if using metal skewers. Preheat grill to 350° to 400° (medium-high) heat. Remove steak and potatoes from marinades, discarding marinades. Thread steak onto 6 skewers, leaving a ⅛ inch space between pieces. Sprinkle with desired amount of salt and pepper.

4. Grill potatoes and steak at the same time, covered with grill lid, 6 to 7 minutes on each side or until steak reaches desired degree of doneness and potatoes are golden brown, basting potatoes and steak with melted butter with each turn. Toss together arugula, next 5 ingredients, and 2 Tbsp. vinaigrette. Serve kabobs with arugula salad and remaining vinaigrette.

**BÉARNAISE VINAIGRETTE**
MAKES ABOUT 2 CUPS
HANDS-ON 5 MIN.
TOTAL 5 MIN.

Whisk together ¾ cup white wine vinegar; ¼ cup chopped fresh tarragon; ¼ cup fresh lemon juice; 3 shallots, minced; 2 garlic cloves, minced; 1 Tbsp. Dijon mustard; 2 tsp. sugar; 1 ½ tsp. salt; and 1 tsp. black pepper in a bowl until blended. Add ½ cup canola oil and ½ cup olive oil, 1 at a time, in a slow, steady stream, whisking constantly until mixture is smooth.

# Enchilada Casserole

## Texas-Style

MAKES 6 SERVINGS
HANDS-ON 25 MIN.
TOTAL 45 MIN.

1 lb. ground chuck
½ medium-size red onion, chopped
1 (4-oz.) can diced green chiles
12 (6-inch) fajita-size corn tortillas, cut into 1-inch
    pieces
1 (10 ¾-oz.) can cream of mushroom soup
1 (2 ¼-oz.) can sliced black olives, drained
1 cup mild enchilada sauce
½ cup sour cream
2 cups (8 oz.) shredded sharp Cheddar cheese
Toppings: shredded lettuce, finely chopped
    red onion

1. Preheat oven to 400°. Lightly grease an 11- x 7-inch baking dish. Cook first 3 ingredients in a large skillet over medium-high heat, stirring often, 6 to 8 minutes or until beef crumbles and is no longer pink. Drain well.

2. Place beef mixture in a large bowl. Stir in tortilla pieces, next 4 ingredients, and 1 cup cheese; spoon mixture into prepared baking dish. Sprinkle with remaining 1 cup cheese.

3. Bake at 400° for 20 to 25 minutes or until bubbly. Serve casserole with desired toppings.

## Make It Easy:

*This dish uses pantry staples such as canned green chiles, soup, and enchilada sauce to bring it together even faster.*

# Beef & Bacon Pizza

MAKES 8 SERVINGS
HANDS-ON 20 MIN.
TOTAL 35 MIN.

½ lb. lean ground beef
1¼ cups sliced onion
3 garlic cloves, minced
1 tsp. chopped fresh rosemary
½ tsp. pepper
Plain yellow cornmeal
1 lb. prepared pizza dough, at room temperature
½ cup marinara sauce
1 cup (4 oz.) part-skim mozzarella cheese, shredded
   and divided
½ cup (2 oz.) freshly grated Parmesan cheese
4 slices center-cut bacon, cooked and crumbled

*1.* Preheat oven to 450°.

*2.* Cook beef in a large nonstick skillet over medium-high heat until beef crumbles and is no longer pink. Drain. Add onion to pan; sauté 6 minutes or until tender and beginning to brown. Add garlic; sauté 1 minute. Add beef, rosemary, and pepper to onion mixture.

*3.* Sprinkle cornmeal on a large baking sheet. Roll dough into a 12-inch circle; place on prepared baking sheet. Spread sauce over dough, leaving a ½-inch border. Sprinkle with ½ cup mozzarella cheese. Spread beef mixture over cheese. Top with remaining mozzarella and Parmesan cheeses. Sprinkle with bacon.

*4.* Bake at 450° for 15 minutes or until crust is golden.

## Make It Easy:

**Cut the onion and mince the garlic while the oven preheats.**

# Easy Lasagna

MAKES 6 TO 8 SERVINGS
HANDS-ON 20 MIN.
TOTAL 1 HOUR, 30 MIN.

1 (1-lb.) package mild Italian sausage,
    casings removed
1 (15-oz.) container low-fat ricotta cheese
¼ cup jarred refrigerated pesto sauce
1 large egg, lightly beaten
2 (24-oz.) jars tomato-and-basil pasta sauce
9 no-boil lasagna noodles
4 cups (16 oz.) shredded Italian three-cheese blend
    or mozzarella cheese

*1.* Preheat oven to 350°. Lightly grease a 13- x 9-inch baking dish. Cook sausage in a large skillet over medium heat, stirring often, 8 to 10 minutes or until meat crumbles and is no longer pink; drain sausage well on paper towels.

*2.* Stir together ricotta cheese, pesto, and egg.

*3.* Spread half of 1 jar pasta sauce into prepared baking dish. Layer with 3 lasagna noodles (noodles should not touch each other or sides of dish), half of ricotta mixture, half of sausage, 1 cup three-cheese blend, and remaining half of 1 jar pasta sauce. Repeat layers using 3 lasagna noodles, remaining ricotta mixture, remaining sausage, and 1 cup three-cheese blend. Top with remaining 3 noodles and second jar of pasta sauce, covering noodles completely. Sprinkle with remaining 2 cups three-cheese blend.

*4.* Bake, covered, at 350° for 40 minutes. Uncover and bake 15 more minutes or until cheese is melted and edges are lightly browned and bubbly. Let stand 15 minutes.

Note: We tested with Classico Tomato & Basil pasta sauce.

## Make It Easy:

**Use no-boil noodles to save the step of preparing the pasta.**

# Pizza Supreme

MAKES 6 SERVINGS
HANDS-ON 20 MIN.
TOTAL 35 MIN.

1 (16-oz.) package frozen pizza crusts, thawed
Cooking spray
2 tsp. olive oil
1 (4-oz.) link sweet turkey Italian sausage, casing
    removed
1 cup sliced fresh mushrooms
1 cup thinly sliced red bell pepper
1 cup thinly sliced orange bell pepper
1 cup thinly sliced red onion
¼ tsp. dried crushed red pepper
3 garlic cloves, thinly sliced
¾ cup lower-sodium marinara sauce
5 oz. fresh mozzarella cheese, thinly sliced

1. Preheat oven to 500°.

2. Roll 1 pizza crust into a 14-inch circle on a lightly floured surface. Place crust on a 14-inch pizza pan or baking sheet coated with cooking spray.

3. Heat oil in a large nonstick skillet over medium-high heat. Add sausage to pan; cook 2 minutes or until sausage crumbles and is no longer pink. Add mushrooms, bell peppers, onion, crushed red pepper, and garlic; sauté 4 minutes, stirring occasionally. Drain.

4. Spread sauce over crust, leaving a 1-inch border. Arrange cheese over sauce. Arrange sausage mixture evenly over cheese. Bake at 500° for 15 minutes or until crust and cheese are browned.

## Kitchen Note:

*For the fastest browning, put a rack in the lowest position with a pizza stone if you have one. Preheat the oven; you want it as hot as it can get for a crisp crust.*

# Red Beans & Rice

MAKES 10 TO 12 SERVINGS
HANDS-ON 30 MIN.
TOTAL 3 HOURS, 45 MIN.

1 (16-oz.) package dried red kidney beans
1 lb. mild smoked sausage, cut into ¼-inch-thick slices
1 (½-lb.) smoked ham hock, cut in half
¼ cup vegetable oil
3 celery ribs, diced
1 medium-size yellow onion, diced
1 green bell pepper, diced
3 bay leaves
3 garlic cloves, chopped
2 Tbsp. salt-free Cajun seasoning
1 tsp. kosher salt
1 tsp. dried thyme
1 tsp. freshly ground black pepper
3 (32-oz.) containers low-sodium chicken broth

1. Place beans in a large Dutch oven; add water to 2 inches above beans. Boil 1 minute; cover, remove from heat, and let stand 1 hour. Drain.

2. Cook sausage and ham hock in hot oil in Dutch oven over medium-high heat 8 to 10 minutes or until browned. Drain sausage and ham hock on paper towels, reserving 2 Tbsp. drippings. Add celery and next 8 ingredients to drippings; cook over low heat, stirring occasionally, 15 minutes.

3. Add broth, beans, sausage, and ham hock to Dutch oven. Bring to a simmer. Cook, stirring occasionally, 2 hours or until beans are tender. Discard ham hock and bay leaves.

## Simple Swap:

*For an extra kick, use spicy sausage instead of mild and add a few dashes of hot sauce before serving.*

## Simple Swap:

Substitute chicken for the sausage. Prepare recipe as directed through Step 3. Stir in $\frac{1}{2}$ to $\frac{3}{4}$ lb. peeled and deveined, medium-size raw shrimp. Cook 5 minutes or until the shrimp turn pink.

# Chicken Gumbo
## with Roasted Potatoes

**MAKES 10 CUPS**
**HANDS-ON 45 MIN.**
**TOTAL 3 HOURS, 5 MIN., INCLUDING POTATOES**

1 lb. andouille sausage, cut into ¼-inch-thick slices
½ cup peanut oil
¾ cup all-purpose flour
1 large onion, coarsely chopped
1 red bell pepper, coarsely chopped
1 cup thinly sliced celery
2 garlic cloves, minced
2 tsp. Cajun seasoning
⅛ tsp. ground red pepper (optional)
1 (48-oz.) container chicken broth
2 lb. skinned and boned chicken breasts
Roasted Potatoes
Toppings: chopped fresh parsley, cooked and
    crumbled bacon, hot sauce

1. Cook sausage in a large skillet over medium heat, stirring often, 7 minutes or until browned. Remove sausage; drain and pat dry with paper towels.

2. Heat oil in a stainless steel Dutch oven over medium heat; gradually whisk in flour, and cook, whisking constantly, 18 to 20 minutes or until flour is caramel-colored. (Do not burn mixture.) Reduce heat to low, and cook, whisking constantly, until mixture is milk chocolate-colored and texture is smooth (about 2 minutes).

3. Increase heat to medium. Stir in onion, next 4 ingredients, and, if desired, ground red pepper. Cook, stirring constantly, 3 minutes. Gradually stir in chicken broth; add chicken and sausage.

4. Increase heat to medium-high, and bring to a boil. Reduce heat to low, and simmer, stirring occasionally, 1 hour and 30 minutes to 1 hour and 40 minutes or until chicken is done. Shred chicken into large pieces with 2 forks. Place potatoes in serving bowls. Spoon gumbo over potatoes. Serve with desired toppings.

**ROASTED POTATOES**
**MAKES 6 TO 8 SERVINGS**
**HANDS-ON 10 MIN.**
**TOTAL 50 MIN.**

3 lb. baby red potatoes, quartered
1 Tbsp. peanut oil
1 tsp. kosher salt

Preheat oven to 450°. Stir together all ingredients in a large bowl. Place red potatoes in a single layer in a lightly greased 15- x 10-inch jelly-roll pan. Bake 40 to 45 minutes or until tender and browned, stirring twice.

# Jambalaya
## with Chicken and Sausage

MAKES 6 SERVINGS
HANDS-ON 30 MIN.
TOTAL 1 HOUR

1 whole deli-roasted (rotisserie) chicken
1 lb. smoked sausage, cut into ¼-inch-thick slices
1 medium-size green bell pepper, chopped
1 small onion, chopped
2 (10-oz.) cans mild diced tomatoes and green chiles
1 (14-oz.) can chicken broth
1 tsp. garlic powder
1 tsp. Cajun seasoning
2 cups uncooked long-grain rice

1. Remove chicken from bones; cut chicken into bite-size pieces, and set aside.

2. Cook sausage in a Dutch oven over medium heat, stirring occasionally, 5 minutes. Add bell pepper and onion; cook, stirring occasionally, 3 minutes or until vegetables are tender.

3. Stir in tomatoes and green chiles, broth, 1 cup water, garlic powder, and Cajun seasoning; bring to a boil, stirring occasionally. Stir in chicken and rice. Cover, reduce heat, and simmer 30 minutes or until rice is tender.

## Make It Easy:

*Use a deli rotisserie chicken and canned ingredients to make quick work of this Louisiana favorite.*

# Chicken Crêpes
## with Swiss Cheese Sauce

MAKES 4 TO 6 SERVINGS
HANDS-ON 20 MIN.
TOTAL 55 MIN., INCLUDING SAUCE

1 (12-oz.) jar roasted red bell peppers, drained
Swiss Cheese Sauce
3 cups finely chopped cooked chicken
1 (6-oz.) package fresh baby spinach, chopped
1 cup (4 oz.) shredded Swiss cheese
¼ cup chopped fresh basil
1 garlic clove, pressed
1 tsp. seasoned pepper
8 egg roll wrappers
Garnish: fresh basil leaves

1. Preheat oven to 350°.

2. Process peppers in a blender until smooth, stopping to scrape down sides as needed. Pour into 4 lightly greased 7- x 4 ½-inch baking dishes.

3. Prepare Swiss Cheese Sauce. Stir together chicken, next 5 ingredients, and 1 cup Swiss Cheese Sauce.

4. Divide chicken mixture among wrappers, spooning down centers; gently roll up. Place, seam sides down, over red peppers in baking dishes. Top with remaining Swiss Cheese Sauce. Cover with aluminum foil.

5. Bake, covered, at 350° for 15 minutes or until thoroughly heated and bubbly.

SWISS CHEESE SAUCE
MAKES ABOUT 4 CUPS
HANDS-ON 20 MIN.
TOTAL 20 MIN.

⅓ cup dry vermouth
1 garlic clove, pressed
3 cups half-and-half
3 Tbsp. cornstarch
1 tsp. table salt
½ tsp. black pepper
2 cups (8 oz.) shredded Swiss cheese

Bring vermouth and garlic to a boil in a large skillet over medium-high heat; reduce heat to medium-low, and simmer 7 to 10 minutes or until vermouth is reduced to 1 Tbsp. Whisk together half-and-half and cornstarch. Whisk salt, pepper, and half-and-half mixture into vermouth mixture; bring to a boil over medium-high heat, whisking constantly. Boil, whisking constantly, 1 minute or until mixture is thickened. Add cheese; reduce heat to low, and simmer, whisking constantly, 1 minute or until cheese is melted and sauce is smooth. Remove from heat, and use immediately.

## Make It Easy:

*This recipe uses egg roll wrappers instead of crêpes, making it ideal for a quick weeknight dinner.*

# Mac and Cheese
## with King Ranch Chicken

MAKES 6 SERVINGS
HANDS-ON 20 MIN.
TOTAL 45 MIN.

½ (16-oz.) package cellentani (corkscrew) pasta
2 Tbsp. butter
1 medium onion, diced
1 green bell pepper, diced
1 (10-oz.) can diced tomatoes and green chiles
1 (8-oz.) package processed cheese, cubed
3 cups chopped cooked chicken
1 (10 ¾-oz.) can cream of chicken soup
½ cup sour cream
1 tsp. chili powder
½ tsp. ground cumin
1½ cups (6 oz.) shredded Cheddar cheese

*1.* Preheat oven to 350°. Prepare pasta according to package directions.

*2.* Meanwhile, melt butter in a large Dutch oven over medium-high heat. Add onion and bell pepper, and sauté 5 minutes or until tender. Stir in tomatoes and green chiles and processed cheese; cook, stirring constantly, 2 minutes or until cheese melts. Stir in chicken, next 4 ingredients, and hot cooked pasta until blended. Spoon mixture into a lightly greased 10-inch cast-iron skillet or 11- x 7-inch baking dish; sprinkle with shredded Cheddar cheese.

*3.* Bake at 350° for 25 to 30 minutes or until bubbly.

## Macaroni & Cheese

The sturdy simplicity of macaroni and cheese offers a happy reminder that no matter how rough the day has been, there is comfort to be found. Here are some tips for making the perfect mac and cheese.

**PASTA SECRETS:** Properly season the water before you boil the pasta. And barely undercook the pasta so that it will be slightly moist before baking.

**SAY CHEESE:** Use the best quality cheese that you can find. Grate the cheese yourself rather than purchasing preshredded cheese.

**ADD A LITTLE SOMETHING:** Fresh vegetables, bacon, and deli roasted chicken are just a few examples of the host of ingredients that can add a whole new flavor to this classic dish.

**Make It Easy:**

*Make the pasta up to two days ahead, and drain. Toss with a few drops of olive oil, and cool. Place in a plastic zip-top freezer bag, and refrigerate until ready to use.*

# Chicken Stir-fry

MAKES 4 SERVINGS
HANDS-ON 30 MIN.
TOTAL 30 MIN.

1 lb. skinned and boned chicken breasts, cut into
thin strips
½ tsp. table salt
¼ cup cornstarch
4 Tbsp. vegetable oil, divided
½ lb. Broccolini, cut into 1-inch pieces
1 cup chicken broth, divided
1 red bell pepper, cut into thin strips
1 small yellow squash, thinly sliced into half moons
¼ cup sliced green onions
2 tsp. cornstarch
1 Tbsp. fresh lime juice
1½ tsp. soy sauce
1 tsp. Asian chili-garlic sauce
Hot cooked rice

1. Sprinkle chicken with salt; toss with ¼ cup
cornstarch.

2. Stir-fry chicken in 3 Tbsp. hot oil in a large skillet or
wok over medium-high heat 5 to 6 minutes or until
golden brown and done. Transfer to a plate, using
a slotted spoon; keep warm. Add Broccolini and
¼ cup broth; cover and cook 1 to 2 minutes or until
crisp-tender. Transfer to plate with chicken, using
slotted spoon.

3. Add remaining 1 Tbsp. oil to skillet. Sauté bell
pepper and next 2 ingredients in hot oil 2 minutes
or until crisp-tender.

4. Whisk together 2 tsp. cornstarch and remaining
¾ cup broth until cornstarch dissolves. Add broth
mixture, chicken, and Broccolini (with any accumu-
lated juices) to bell pepper mixture in skillet. Cook,
stirring often, 1 minute or until liquid thickens. Stir in
lime juice and next 2 ingredients. Serve over hot
cooked rice.

## Simple Swap:

*Use fresh green beans as an
alternative to Broccolini.*

**Make It Easy:**

Prep this recipe a day ahead and then fry it at your convenience.

# Sweet Tea-Brined

## Fried Chicken

MAKES 6 TO 8 SERVINGS
HANDS-ON 50 MIN.
TOTAL 2 HOURS, 20 MIN., PLUS 1 DAY FOR BRINING

2 family-size tea bags
½ cup firmly packed light brown sugar
¼ cup kosher salt
1 small sweet onion, thinly sliced
1 lemon, thinly sliced
4 garlic cloves, halved
1 Tbsp. cracked black pepper
2 cups ice cubes
1 (3 ½-lb.) cut-up whole chicken
2 cups self-rising flour
1 cup self-rising white cornmeal mix
2 Tbsp. freshly ground black pepper
2 tsp. table salt
1 tsp. ground red pepper
Vegetable oil

*1.* Bring 4 cups water to a boil in a 3-qt. heavy sauce-pan; add tea bags. Remove from heat; cover and steep 10 minutes.

*2.* Discard tea bags. Stir in brown sugar and next 5 ingredients, stirring until sugar dissolves. Cool completely (about 45 minutes); stir in ice. (Mixture should be cold before adding to chicken.)

*3.* Cut chicken breasts in half crosswise. Place tea mixture and all chicken pieces in a large zip-top plastic freezer bag; seal. Chill 24 hours.

*4.* Remove chicken from marinade, discarding marinade. Drain chicken well.

*5.* Whisk together flour and next 4 ingredients in a medium bowl. Spoon 1 cup flour mixture into a brown paper bag or large zip-top plastic freezer bag. Place 1 piece of chicken in bag; seal and shake to coat. Remove chicken, and transfer to a wire rack. Repeat procedure with remaining chicken, adding more flour mixture to bag as needed. Let chicken stand 30 minutes to form a crust.

*6.* Pour oil to depth of 1 ½ inches into a cast-iron Dutch oven; heat over medium heat to 325°. Fry chicken, in batches, 15 to 22 minutes or until browned and done, turning occasionally. Drain on a wire rack over paper towels.

Note: If using a 12-inch-wide (2 ¼-inch-deep) cast-iron skillet, pour oil to depth of 1 inch.

## Sweet Tea

Our Test Kitchen has a few secrets to making this Southern specialty.

**ICE IDEA:** Instead of regular ice cubes, use tea frozen in an ice cube tray.

**FRESHEN UP:** Fresh mint sprigs, lemon slices, and lime wedges all make nice garnishes.

**A LITTLE SUGAR:** Teas made with no-calorie sweeteners (versus sugar) tend to get sweeter when stored.

# Chicken Cobblers

MAKES 4 SERVINGS
HANDS-ON 35 MIN.
TOTAL 50 MIN.

6 Tbsp. melted butter, divided
4 cups cubed sourdough rolls
⅓ cup grated Parmesan cheese
2 Tbsp. chopped fresh parsley
2 medium-size sweet onions, sliced
1 (8-oz.) package sliced fresh mushrooms
1 cup white wine
1 (10 ¾-oz.) can cream of mushroom soup
½ cup drained and chopped jarred roasted red bell
    peppers
2 ½ cups shredded cooked chicken

*1.* Preheat oven to 400°.

*2.* Toss 4 Tbsp. melted butter with next 3 ingredients; set aside.

*3.* Sauté onions in remaining 2 Tbsp. butter in a large skillet over medium-high heat 15 minutes or until golden brown. Add mushrooms, and sauté 5 minutes.

*4.* Stir in wine and next 3 ingredients; cook, stirring constantly, 5 minutes or until bubbly. Spoon mixture into a lightly greased 9-inch square baking dish; top with bread mixture.

*5.* Bake at 400° for 15 minutes or until golden brown.

## Kitchen Note:

**Buttery cubes of sourdough rolls make a quick and crunchy topping for this speedy twist on chicken pot pie.**

# Stovetop Chicken
## with Biscuit Topping

MAKES 6 TO 8 SERVINGS
HANDS-ON 35 MIN.
TOTAL 35 MIN.

8 frozen buttermilk biscuits
1 small sweet onion, diced
1 Tbsp. canola oil
1 (8-oz.) package sliced fresh mushrooms
4 cups chopped cooked chicken
1 (10¾-oz.) can reduced-fat cream of mushroom soup
1 cup low-sodium chicken broth
½ cup dry white wine
½ (8-oz.) package ⅓-less-fat cream cheese, cubed
½ (0.7-oz.) envelope Italian dressing mix (about 2 tsp.)
1 cup frozen baby peas, thawed

1. Bake biscuits according to package directions.

2. Meanwhile, sauté onion in hot oil in a large skillet over medium-high heat 5 minutes or until golden. Add mushrooms, and sauté 5 minutes or until tender. Stir in chicken and next 5 ingredients; cook, stirring frequently, 5 minutes or until cheese is melted and mixture is thoroughly heated. Stir in peas, and cook 2 minutes. Spoon chicken mixture over hot split biscuits.

## Make It Easy:

*Update your chicken pot pie with this recipe that includes sautéed mushrooms and baby peas. Frozen biscuits make a quick and easy "crust" that your family will love.*

# Chicken Pot Pie

**MAKES 6 TO 8 SERVINGS**
**HANDS-ON 30 MIN.**
**TOTAL 1 HOUR, 30 MIN.**

**CHICKEN PIE FILLING**
⅓ cup butter
⅓ cup all-purpose flour
1 ½ cups chicken broth
1 ½ cups milk
1 ½ tsp. Creole seasoning
2 Tbsp. butter
1 large sweet onion, diced
1 (8-oz.) package sliced fresh mushrooms
4 cups shredded cooked chicken
2 cups frozen cubed hash browns
1 cup matchstick carrots
1 cup frozen small sweet peas
⅓ cup chopped fresh parsley

**PASTRY CRUST**
1 (14.1-oz.) package refrigerated piecrusts
1 egg white

*1.* Prepare Filling: Preheat oven to 350°. Melt ⅓ cup butter in a large saucepan over medium heat; add all-purpose flour, and cook, whisking constantly, 1 minute. Gradually add chicken broth and milk; cook, whisking constantly, 6 to 7 minutes or until thickened and bubbly. Remove from heat, and stir in Creole seasoning.

*2.* Melt 2 Tbsp. butter in a large Dutch oven over medium-high heat; add onion and mushrooms, and sauté 10 minutes or until tender. Stir in chicken, next 4 ingredients, and sauce.

*3.* Prepare Crust: Place 1 piecrust in a lightly greased 10-inch cast-iron skillet. Spoon chicken mixture over piecrust, and top with remaining piecrust.

*4.* Whisk egg white until foamy; brush top of piecrust with egg white. Cut 4 to 5 slits in top of pie for steam to escape.

*5.* Bake at 350° for 1 hour to 1 hour and 5 minutes or until golden brown and bubbly.

## Make It Easy:

*If you don't have time to simmer a whole chicken, substitute an equal amount of canned broth and the meat from a rotisserie chicken from the grocery store.*

# Oven-Baked Pilau

## with Chicken and Collards

MAKES 6 TO 8 SERVINGS.
HANDS-ON 40 MIN.
TOTAL 1 HOUR, 5 MIN.

6 oz. Cajun smoked sausage, diced
1½ lb. skinned and boned chicken thighs, cubed
1¼ tsp. kosher salt
½ tsp. freshly ground black pepper
1 Tbsp. olive oil
1 cup chopped sweet onion
1 cup chopped celery
1 cup chopped carrot
2 garlic cloves, minced
3 cups organic vegetable broth
4 cups firmly packed chopped fresh collard greens
2 cups uncooked basmati rice
½ tsp. dried crushed red pepper

*1.* Preheat oven to 350°. Cook sausage in a Dutch oven over medium-high heat, stirring often, 5 to 7 minutes or until browned. Remove sausage using a slotted spoon; reserve drippings in Dutch oven. Drain sausage on paper towels.

*2.* Sprinkle chicken with salt and pepper. Add oil to hot drippings in Dutch oven, and cook chicken in hot drippings over medium-high heat, stirring occasionally, 8 to 10 minutes or until done. Add onion and next 3 ingredients. Cook, stirring often, 5 to 7 minutes or until onion is tender. Stir in broth, next 3 ingredients, and sausage.

*3.* Bring mixture to a boil over medium-high heat. Remove from heat; cover.

*4.* Bake pilau at 350° for 20 to 25 minutes or until liquid is absorbed, stirring halfway through. Serve pilau immediately.

## Kitchen Note:

*Quick-cooking basmati rice helps turn this recipe into dinner fast and stays fluffy throughout the entire cooking process.*

**Kitchen Note:**

*Smoky cubes of brined city ham and salty bits of country ham give this main-course mac its name and savory appeal. Pasta enrobed in a creamy sauce and melting pockets of gooey cheese take it over the top.*

# Mac and Cheese

## from the City and Country

MAKES 8 TO 10 SERVINGS
HANDS-ON 40 MIN.
TOTAL 1 HOUR 25 MIN.

12 oz. elbow macaroni or
    cavatappi pasta
4 cups diced smoked, fully cooked ham
1 cup diced country ham
2 Tbsp. vegetable oil
6 Tbsp. butter
⅓ cup grated onion
2 tsp. dry mustard
½ tsp. kosher salt
¼ tsp. freshly ground black pepper
¼ tsp. freshly grated nutmeg
⅛ tsp. ground red pepper
5 Tbsp. all-purpose flour
3½ cups milk
1¾ cups heavy cream
2 tsp. prepared horseradish
2 tsp. Worcestershire sauce
2 cups (8 oz.) shredded extra-sharp Cheddar cheese
2 cups diced Gruyère or Swiss cheese
1½ cups soft, fresh breadcrumbs (about
    4 white bread slices)
2 Tbsp. butter, melted
1 Tbsp. minced fresh chives

1. Preheat oven to 350°. Prepare pasta according to package directions for al dente.

2. Stir together smoked ham and country ham. Sauté half of ham mixture in 1 Tbsp. hot oil in a large skillet 7 to 8 minutes or until lightly browned. Repeat with remaining ham mixture and oil.

3. Melt 6 Tbsp. butter in a large saucepan over medium heat. Add onion and next 5 ingredients, and sauté 30 seconds or until fragrant. Add flour, and cook, stirring constantly, 2 minutes or until golden brown and smooth. Gradually whisk in milk and cream, and bring to a boil, whisking occasionally. Reduce heat to medium-low, and simmer, whisking constantly, 5 minutes or until slightly thickened and mixture coats a spoon. Stir in horseradish and Worcestershire sauce. Remove from heat, and stir in Cheddar cheese until melted. Stir in pasta, ham, and Gruyère; pour into a lightly greased 13- x 9-inch baking dish.

4. Process breadcrumbs and 2 Tbsp. melted butter in a food processor 6 to 7 seconds to combine. Sprinkle over pasta mixture.

5. Bake on an aluminum foil-lined jelly-roll pan at 350° for 30 minutes or until bubbly and golden. Remove from oven to a wire rack, and cool 15 minutes. Top with chives.

Note: We tested with Cracker Barrel Extra Sharp Cheddar.

## Simple Swap:

*Farfalle and penne can be used in place of the bow-tie pasta.*

# Chicken Pasta

MAKES 6 SERVINGS
HANDS-ON 30 MIN.
TOTAL 30 MIN.

1 (12-oz.) package farfalle (bow-tie) pasta
5 Tbsp. butter, divided
1 medium onion, chopped
1 medium-size red bell pepper, chopped
1 (8-oz.) package fresh mushrooms, quartered
⅓ cup all-purpose flour
3 cups chicken broth
2 cups milk
3 cups chopped cooked chicken
1 cup (4 oz.) shredded Parmesan cheese
1 tsp. black pepper
½ tsp. table salt
Toppings: toasted sliced almonds, chopped fresh
      flat-leaf parsley, shredded Parmesan cheese

*1.* Prepare pasta according to package directions.
Meanwhile, melt 2 Tbsp. butter in a Dutch oven
over medium heat. Add onion and bell pepper;
sauté 5 minutes or until tender. Add mushrooms;
sauté 4 minutes. Remove from Dutch oven.

*2.* Melt remaining 3 Tbsp. butter in Dutch oven over
low heat; whisk in flour until smooth. Cook,
whisking constantly, 1 minute. Gradually whisk in
chicken broth and milk; cook over medium heat,
whisking constantly, 5 to 7 minutes or until thickened and bubbly.

*3.* Stir chicken, sautéed vegetables, and hot cooked
pasta into sauce. Add cheese, pepper, and salt.
Serve with desired toppings.

# Salmon Kabobs

MAKES 6 SERVINGS
HANDS-ON 30 MIN.
TOTAL 3 HOURS, 30 MIN.

3 tsp. ground coriander
2 tsp. ground cumin
1 tsp. salt
½ tsp. ground red pepper
1 (2 ¼-lb.) whole skinless salmon fillet,
    cut into 1-inch cubes
1 cup plain yogurt
⅓ cup finely chopped pickled okra
1 Tbsp. olive oil
2 tsp. chopped fresh dill
1½ tsp. fresh lemon juice
6 (12-inch) wooden or metal skewers
3 Kirby cucumbers
12 grape tomatoes
Garnish: chopped fresh dill

*1.* Stir together first 4 ingredients in a bowl; transfer to a large zip-top plastic freezer bag. Add salmon, seal bag, and turn gently to coat. Chill 3 hours, turning occasionally.

*2.* Meanwhile, stir together yogurt and next 4 ingredients; cover and chill until ready to serve. Soak wooden skewers in water 30 minutes. (Omit if using metal skewers.)

*3.* Preheat grill to 350° to 400° (medium-high) heat. Scrape outside of cucumbers lengthwise using tines of a fork, scoring skin all the way around, cut into half moons.

*4.* Remove salmon from marinade, discarding marinade. Thread salmon, cucumbers, and tomatoes alternately onto skewers, leaving a ⅛-inch space between pieces.

*5.* Grill, covered with grill lid, 5 to 6 minutes on each side or to desired degree of doneness. Serve with yogurt mixture. Garnish kabobs and yogurt mixture with chopped fresh dill.

## Make It Easy:

**Snip the ends of the dill with kitchen shears and continue to trim until chopped.**

# Shrimp Kabobs
## with Watermelon

**MAKES 6 SERVINGS**
**HANDS-ON 40 MIN.**
**TOTAL 1 HOUR, 15 MIN., INCLUDING MARINADE**

36 unpeeled, jumbo raw shrimp (about 2 lb.)
12 (12-inch) wooden or metal skewers
Cilantro-Lime Marinade
12 oz. halloumi cheese, cut into 1 ½-inch cubes
24 (2-inch) watermelon cubes
3 Tbsp. fresh cilantro leaves, torn
3 Tbsp. fresh mint leaves, torn

*1.* Peel shrimp, leaving tails on; devein, if desired.

*2.* Soak wooden skewers in water 30 minutes. (Omit if using metal skewers.)

*3.* Meanwhile, combine shrimp and ½ cup Cilantro-Lime Marinade in a large zip-top plastic freezer bag. Combine cheese and ⅓ cup Cilantro-Lime Marinade in another large zip-top plastic freezer bag. Seal bags, turning to coat; chill 30 minutes, turning occasionally.

*4.* Preheat grill to 350° to 400° (medium-high) heat. Remove shrimp and cheese from marinades, discarding marinades. Thread shrimp, watermelon, and cheese alternately onto skewers, leaving a ⅛-inch space between pieces.

*5.* Grill kabobs, covered with grill lid, 4 to 5 minutes on each side or just until shrimp turn pink. Sprinkle with cilantro and mint. Serve with remaining Cilantro-Lime Marinade.

**CILANTRO-LIME MARINADE**

**MAKES 2 CUPS**
**HANDS-ON 5 MIN.**
**TOTAL 5 MIN.**

Whisk together 1 cup red wine vinegar; ⅓ cup chopped fresh cilantro; 2 Tbsp. seeded and minced jalapeño pepper; 1 Tbsp. sugar; 2 Tbsp. lime zest; ¼ cup fresh lime juice; 2 Tbsp. Dijon mustard; 2 garlic cloves, pressed; and 1 tsp. kosher salt until blended. Add 1 cup canola oil in a slow, steady stream, whisking constantly until smooth.

## Simple Swap:

*Halloumi cheese is a favorite for grilling because the outside of the cheese gets beautifully brown and crisp, while the inside stays tender. Mozzarella cheese can be substituted.*

# Breakfast in a Skillet

MAKES 6 SERVINGS
HANDS-ON 20 MIN.
TOTAL 45 MIN., NOT INCLUDING BISCUITS

1 lb. ground pork sausage
1 cup diced onion
2 garlic cloves, minced
2 cups crumbled homemade biscuits
6 oz. freshly grated extra-sharp Cheddar cheese, (1½ cups)
1 cup grape tomatoes, quartered
⅛ tsp. freshly ground black pepper
6 large eggs

1. Preheat oven to 350°. Heat a 10-inch cast-iron skillet in oven 5 minutes.

2. Meanwhile, cook sausage, onion, and garlic in a large, lightly greased skillet over medium heat, stirring frequently, 10 minutes or until sausage is browned and onion is tender. Transfer to a large bowl. Add biscuit crumbles and next 3 ingredients. Stir until blended. Transfer to hot cast-iron skillet.

3. Make 6 indentations in sausage mixture using back of a spoon. Break 1 egg into each indentation.

4. Bake at 350° for 23 to 25 minutes or just until eggs are set. Serve immediately.

## Simple Swap:

**Using precooked sausage crumbles or premade biscuits will cut this recipe's hands-on time.**

# Tomato Pie
## with Bacon and Cheddar

MAKES 6 TO 8 SERVINGS
HANDS-ON 45 MIN.
TOTAL 3 HOURS

**CRUST**
2 ¼ cups self-rising soft-wheat flour
    (such as White Lily)
1 cup cold butter, cut up
8 cooked bacon slices, chopped
¾ cup sour cream

**FILLING**
2 ¾ lb. assorted large tomatoes, divided
2 tsp. kosher salt, divided
1 ½ cups (6 oz.) freshly shredded extra-sharp
    Cheddar cheese
½ cup freshly shredded Parmigiano-Reggiano
    cheese
½ cup mayonnaise
1 large egg, lightly beaten
2 Tbsp. fresh dill sprigs
1 Tbsp. chopped fresh chives
1 Tbsp. chopped fresh flat-leaf parsley
1 Tbsp. apple cider vinegar
1 green onion, thinly sliced
2 tsp. sugar
¼ tsp. freshly ground black pepper
1 ½ Tbsp. plain yellow cornmeal

1. Prepare Crust: Place flour in bowl of a heavy-duty electric stand mixer; cut in cold butter with a pastry blender or fork until crumbly. Chill 10 minutes.

2. Add bacon to flour mixture; beat at low speed just until combined. Gradually add sour cream, ¼ cup at a time, beating just until blended after each addition.

3. Spoon mixture onto a heavily floured surface; sprinkle lightly with flour, and knead 3 or 4 times, adding more flour as needed. Roll to a 13-inch round. Gently place dough in a 9-inch fluted tart pan with 2-inch sides and a removable bottom. Press dough into pan; trim off excess dough along edges. Chill 30 minutes.

4. Meanwhile, prepare Filling: Cut 2 lb. tomatoes into ¼-inch-thick slices, and remove seeds. Place tomatoes in a single layer on paper towels; sprinkle with 1 tsp. salt. Let stand 30 minutes.

5. Preheat oven to 425°. Stir together Cheddar cheese, next 10 ingredients, and remaining 1 tsp. salt in a large bowl until combined.

6. Pat tomato slices dry with a paper towel. Sprinkle cornmeal over bottom of crust. Lightly spread ½ cup cheese mixture onto crust; layer with half of tomato slices in slightly overlapping rows. Spread with ½ cup cheese mixture. Repeat layers, using remaining tomato slices and cheese mixture. Cut remaining ¾ lb. tomatoes into ¼-inch-thick slices, and arrange on top of pie.

7. Bake at 425° for 40 to 45 minutes, shielding edges with foil during last 20 minutes to prevent excessive browning. Let stand 1 to 2 hours before serving.

**Make It Easy:**

Use a prepared crust rather than making your own if you are short on time.

# Farmers' Market Pizza

MAKES 6 SERVINGS
HANDS-ON 20 MIN.
TOTAL 2 HOURS, 15 MIN., INCLUDING VEGETABLES

Plain white cornmeal
1 lb. bakery pizza dough
½ to ¾ cup tomato sauce
1 (8-oz.) package sliced fresh mozzarella cheese
¼ lb. mild Italian sausage, cooked and crumbled
1 ½ cups Farmers' Market Roasted Vegetables

*1.* Preheat oven to 500°. Heat a pizza stone or baking sheet in oven 30 minutes.

*2.* Meanwhile, lightly dust a second baking sheet with cornmeal. Stretch pizza dough into a 12- to 14-inch circle on baking sheet.

*3.* Spread tomato sauce over dough. Top with mozzarella slices and Italian sausage. Arrange Farmers' Market Roasted Vegetables over pizza; season with kosher salt and freshly ground pepper to taste.

*4.* Slide pizza from baking sheet onto hot pizza stone or baking sheet in oven.

*5.* Bake at 500° for 15 minutes or until crust is thoroughly cooked, edges are golden, and cheese is melted.

## FARMERS' MARKET ROASTED VEGETABLES

MAKES 3 CUPS
HANDS-ON 15 MIN.
TOTAL 1 HOUR, 10 MIN.

1 medium eggplant, cut into 1-inch pieces
2 large red bell peppers, cut into 1-inch pieces
1 fennel bulb, cut into ¼-inch slices
3 garlic cloves, thinly sliced
3 Tbsp. extra virgin olive oil
1 tsp. kosher salt
½ tsp. freshly ground black pepper
2 Tbsp. chopped fresh basil
1 Tbsp. white balsamic vinegar

Preheat oven to 450°. Toss together first 7 ingredients in a bowl until coated. Spread eggplant mixture in a single layer in a 15- x 10-inch jelly-roll pan. Bake 45 to 50 minutes or until vegetables are tender and slightly charred, stirring halfway through. Let cool slightly (about 10 minutes). Toss with basil and vinegar. Serve immediately. Store in an airtight container in refrigerator up to 2 days.

## Make It Easy:

*Make a double batch of roasted vegetables and serve one for dinner one night and save the other to top this pizza.*

# 30-Minute Favorites

# Country-Fried Steak

## with Cornmeal Gravy

MAKES 6 SERVINGS
HANDS-ON 15 MIN.
TOTAL 25 MIN., INCLUDING GRAVY

6 (6-oz.) top sirloin steaks, cubed
1 tsp. kosher salt
¼ tsp. freshly ground black pepper
3 cups all-purpose flour
1½ cups finely crushed round buttery crackers
6 Tbsp. chopped fresh marjoram
3 large eggs
2 cups buttermilk
Vegetable oil
Cornmeal Gravy
Garnishes: fresh thyme leaves, freshly ground
    black pepper

*1.* Sprinkle cubed steaks with salt and pepper.
   Combine flour, crackers, and marjoram in a
   shallow dish. Whisk eggs and buttermilk in a bowl.

*2.* Dip steaks in egg mixture; dredge in cracker
   mixture. Repeat procedure.

*3.* Pour oil to depth of 1½ inches into a large heavy
   skillet. Heat to 325°. Fry steaks, in batches, 5 to
   7 minutes on each side or until golden. Drain on
   a wire rack in a jelly-roll pan. Serve with gravy.

**CORNMEAL GRAVY**
MAKES ABOUT 1⅔ CUPS
HANDS-ON 10 MIN.
TOTAL 10 MIN.

½ cup plain red or white cornmeal
½ tsp. salt
½ tsp. freshly ground black pepper
1 tsp. bacon drippings
1 cup buttermilk
1 cup hot water

Cook cornmeal in a heavy skillet over medium-
high heat, stirring constantly, 4 to 5 minutes or until
golden brown. Stir in salt, pepper, and drippings. Stir
together buttermilk and hot water; gradually whisk
into cornmeal mixture. Bring to a boil, whisking
constantly. Reduce heat. Cook, whisking constantly,
until thickened. Whisk in additional buttermilk for
desired consistency.

## Make It Easy:

**Use a food processor to finely
crush the buttery crackers.**

# Grilled Beef Fillets
## with Pecans and Green Bean Ravioli

MAKES 4 SERVINGS
HANDS-ON 20 MIN.
TOTAL 30 MIN.

4 (4-oz.) beef tenderloin fillets
1 tsp. salt
½ tsp. freshly ground black pepper
1 (20-oz.) package refrigerated cheese-filled ravioli
1 (8-oz.) package fresh small green beans
½ cup chopped pecans
½ cup butter
3 garlic cloves, thinly sliced
1 Tbsp. chopped fresh sage
½ cup (2 oz.) shaved Parmesan cheese

*1.* Preheat grill to 350° to 400° (medium-high) heat. Sprinkle fillets with salt and pepper. Grill, covered with grill lid, 5 to 8 minutes on each side or until a meat thermometer inserted into thickest portion registers 145°. Let stand 10 minutes.

*2.* Cook ravioli and green beans in boiling water to cover in a Dutch oven 4 to 5 minutes or until green beans are crisp-tender. Drain.

*3.* Heat pecans in a large nonstick skillet over medium-low heat, stirring often, 2 to 3 minutes or until toasted and fragrant. Remove from skillet; wipe skillet clean. Melt butter in skillet over medium heat. Add garlic, and sauté 5 to 7 minutes or until garlic is caramel colored and butter begins to brown. Remove from heat, and stir in sage, hot pasta mixture, and pecans. Sprinkle with cheese. Serve immediately with fillets.

## Green Beans

Green beans should be bright green and crisp, with only moderate bulges from the beans snuggled inside the pods.

**STORE:** Fresh beans should be washed before being stored in the refrigerator in plastic bags up to 3 or 4 days.

**PREPARE:** Although they are generally cooked, green beans can be eaten raw. Just rinse them and snap them into bite-size pieces.

**COOK:** To retain nutrients, cook green beans a minimal amount of time. They should keep their bright color when cooked.

**Make It Easy:**

*Use convenience products such as refrigerated ravioli and pre-packaged green beans for a quick weeknight dinner.*

# Hamburger Steak
## with Sweet Onion-Mushroom Gravy

MAKES 4 SERVINGS
HANDS-ON 25 MIN.
TOTAL 33 MIN.

2 honey-wheat bread slices
1 lb. ground round
1 large egg, lightly beaten
2 garlic cloves, minced
½ tsp. table salt
½ tsp. freshly ground black pepper
1 (1.2-oz.) envelope brown gravy mix
1 Tbsp. vegetable oil
1 (8-oz.) package sliced fresh mushrooms
1 medium-size sweet onion, halved and thinly sliced

## Make It Easy:

*To make ahead, proceed with Step 1 as directed. Wrap each patty individually in plastic wrap, and place in a large zip-top plastic freezer bag. Freeze up to 3 months. Thaw frozen patties in refrigerator 8 hours; proceed with Steps 2 and 3.*

1. Process bread slices in a food processor 10 seconds or until finely chopped. Place breadcrumbs in a bowl; add ground round and next 4 ingredients. Gently combine until blended, using your hands. Shape into 4 (4-inch) patties.

2. Whisk together brown gravy mix and 1½ cups water.

3. Cook patties in hot oil in a large skillet over medium-high heat 2 minutes on each side or just until browned. Remove from skillet. Add mushrooms and onion to skillet, and sauté 6 minutes or until tender. Stir in prepared gravy, and bring to a light boil. Return patties to skillet, and spoon gravy over each patty. Cover, reduce heat to low, and simmer 8 to 10 minutes.

# Skillet Spaghetti

## with Sausage and Peppers

MAKES 4 SERVINGS
HANDS-ON 30 MIN.
TOTAL 30 MIN.

8 oz. uncooked spaghetti
1 (1-lb.) package mild Italian sausage, casings removed
1 medium onion, cut into eighths
1 medium-size green bell pepper, cut into strips
1 medium-size red or yellow bell pepper, cut into strips
2 to 3 garlic cloves, minced
1 Tbsp. olive oil
1 (28-oz.) can diced tomatoes with basil, garlic, and oregano
¼ tsp. salt
¼ tsp. black pepper
½ cup grated Parmesan cheese
Garnish: Parmesan cheese

1. Prepare pasta according to package directions.

2. Meanwhile, cook sausage in a large Dutch oven over medium-high heat, stirring often, 8 to 10 minutes or until meat crumbles and is no longer pink. Drain sausage well on paper towels; discard drippings.

3. Sauté onion and next 3 ingredients in hot oil in Dutch oven over medium-high heat 5 to 6 minutes or until vegetables are crisp-tender. Stir in tomatoes, salt, and pepper; cook 4 minutes or until thoroughly heated. Stir in sausage, pasta, and cheese. Transfer mixture to serving platter. Serve immediately.

## Make It Easy:

*To freeze ahead, prepare recipe as directed. Cool 30 minutes. Place pasta mixture in a 13- x 9-inch baking dish. Cover with plastic wrap and aluminum foil. Freeze up to 2 months. Thaw in refrigerator 24 hours. Preheat oven to 350°. Discard plastic wrap. Cover with foil, and bake at 350° for 40 to 45 minutes or until thoroughly heated.*

# Virginia Ham Pasta

MAKES 6 TO 8 SERVINGS
HANDS-ON 30 MIN.
TOTAL 30 MIN.

2 (8.8-oz.) packages strozzapreti pasta
¼ lb. country ham, cut into ⅛-inch-thick strips
   (about ¾ cup)
2 Tbsp. olive oil
3 shallots, thinly sliced
8 oz. assorted wild mushrooms, sliced
1 garlic clove, thinly sliced
1 cup Viognier or dry white wine
½ cup frozen sweet peas
⅓ cup coarsely chopped fresh flat-leaf parsley
¼ cup heavy cream
3 Tbsp. butter
¼ tsp. black pepper
1 cup freshly grated pecorino Romano cheese

1. Prepare pasta according to package directions.

2. Meanwhile, sauté ham in hot oil in a large skillet over medium heat 2 minutes or until lightly browned and crisp. Add shallots; sauté 1 minute. Add mushrooms and garlic, and cook, stirring often, 2 minutes or until mushrooms are tender. Stir in wine, and cook 5 minutes or until reduced by half.

3. Add peas, next 4 ingredients, and ½ cup cheese, stirring until cheese begins to melt and cream begins to thicken. Stir in hot cooked pasta, and toss until coated. Serve immediately with remaining ½ cup cheese.

Note: We tested with Jefferson Vineyards Viognier.

## Simple Swap:

If you can't find strozzapreti pasta, use penne rigate.

# BLT Benedict

## with Avocado-Tomato Relish

MAKES 6 SERVINGS
HANDS-ON 23 MIN.
TOTAL 23 MIN.

1 cup halved grape tomatoes
1 avocado, diced
1 Tbsp. chopped fresh basil
1 garlic clove, minced
2 Tbsp. extra virgin olive oil
1 Tbsp. red wine vinegar, divided
6 large eggs
¼ cup mayonnaise
6 (¾-inch-thick) bakery bread slices, toasted
3 cups firmly packed arugula
12 thick bacon slices, cooked

*1.* Combine tomatoes and next 4 ingredients, salt and pepper to taste, and 2 ½ tsp. red wine vinegar in a small bowl.

*2.* Add water to depth of 3 inches in a large saucepan. Bring to a boil; reduce heat, and maintain at a light simmer. Add remaining ½ tsp. red wine vinegar. Break eggs, and slip into water, 1 at a time, as close as possible to surface. Simmer 3 to 5 minutes or to desired degree of doneness. Remove with a slotted spoon. Trim edges, if desired.

*3.* Spread mayonnaise on 1 side of each bread slice. Layer each with ½ cup arugula, 2 bacon slices, and 1 egg. Top with tomato mixture.

## Simple Swap:

**Sunny-side up or sliced boiled eggs would work just as well as poached eggs for this must-try dish.**

# Fried Chicken

## with Pickled Okra Slaw

MAKES 6 SERVINGS
HANDS-ON 30 MIN.
TOTAL 30 MIN.

6 (4-oz.) chicken breast cutlets
1½ tsp. salt, divided
¾ tsp. black pepper, divided
1¼ cups all-purpose flour
30 saltine crackers, crushed
½ tsp. baking powder
2 large eggs, lightly beaten
⅓ cup hot sauce
Peanut oil
½ cup sour cream
½ tsp. sugar
1 (16-oz.) package shredded coleslaw mix
½ cup sliced pickled okra
1 (4-oz.) jar diced pimiento, drained

*1.* Sprinkle chicken with ½ tsp. salt and ½ tsp. pepper. Place ½ cup flour in a shallow dish. Stir together cracker crumbs, baking powder, and remaining ¾ cup flour in a second shallow dish. Whisk together eggs and hot sauce in a third shallow dish. Dredge chicken in flour, dip in egg mixture, and dredge in cracker mixture, pressing to adhere.

*2.* Pour oil to depth of 1 inch into a 10-inch cast-iron skillet; heat to 360°. Fry half of chicken 3 to 4 minutes. Turn and fry 2 to 3 minutes or until golden brown and done. Repeat procedure with remaining half of chicken.

*3.* Stir together sour cream, sugar, and remaining 1 tsp. salt and ¼ tsp. pepper. Toss together coleslaw mix, pickled okra, diced pimiento, and sour cream mixture. Serve slaw and chicken with additional hot sauce.

## Cast-Iron Skillet

How to Season a Cast-Iron Skillet

**Using a stiff scrub brush,** wash with dish soap and hot water; rinse, and dry thoroughly.

**Spread a thin layer** of solid shortening over both the interior and exterior surfaces of the cookware.

**Place the cookware** upside down on a rack in an aluminum foil-lined broiler pan. Bake at 350° for 1 hour. Turn off the oven, leaving the door closed, and allow the cookware to cool completely before removing.

**You will need to repeat** the procedure several times to darken the color of the cookware from brown to black, but it's ready to use after this first seasoning. Once seasoned, never use harsh detergents to clean it or put it in the dishwasher.

# Pecan Chicken
## with Herbed Tortellini

MAKES 4 SERVINGS
HANDS-ON 30 MIN.
TOTAL 30 MIN.

2 (9-oz.) packages refrigerated cheese-filled
    tortellini
4 (4-oz.) chicken breast cutlets
½ tsp. table salt
¼ tsp. freshly ground black pepper
¾ cup finely chopped pecans
1 large egg, lightly beaten
3 Tbsp. olive oil
½ cup butter
3 garlic cloves, thinly sliced
3 Tbsp. chopped fresh basil
3 Tbsp. chopped fresh parsley
¼ cup (1 oz.) shredded Parmesan cheese

*1.* Prepare pasta according to package directions.

*2.* Meanwhile, sprinkle chicken with salt and pepper. Place pecans in a shallow bowl. Place egg in a second bowl. Dip chicken in egg, allowing excess to drip off. Dredge chicken in pecans, pressing firmly to adhere.

*3.* Cook chicken in hot oil in a large nonstick skillet over medium-high heat 2 minutes on each side or until done. Remove from skillet; wipe skillet clean.

*4.* Melt butter in skillet over medium heat. Add garlic, and sauté 5 to 7 minutes or until garlic is caramel colored and butter begins to turn golden brown. Immediately remove from heat, and stir in basil, parsley, and hot cooked tortellini. Sprinkle with cheese. Serve immediately with chicken.

## Make It Easy:

*Use a food processor to quickly chop the pecans. You can chop a big batch and freeze some to use at a later time.*

# Grilled Chicken
## with Fresh Corncakes

MAKES 4 SERVINGS
HANDS-ON 15 MIN.
TOTAL 1 HOUR, 5 MIN.

3 lemons
2 garlic cloves, pressed
⅓ cup olive oil
1 tsp. Dijon mustard
¼ tsp. freshly ground black pepper
1½ tsp. salt, divided
3 skinned and boned chicken breasts
3 ears fresh corn, husks removed
1 Tbsp. olive oil
1 (6-oz.) package buttermilk cornbread mix
¼ cup chopped fresh basil
8 cooked thick hickory-smoked bacon slices
2 cups loosely packed arugula

1. Preheat grill to 350° to 400° (medium-high) heat. Grate zest from lemons to equal 1 Tbsp. Cut lemons in half; squeeze juice from lemons into a measuring cup to equal ¼ cup.

2. Whisk together lemon zest, lemon juice, garlic, next 3 ingredients, and 1 tsp. salt. Reserve ¼ cup lemon mixture. Pour remaining lemon mixture in a large zip-top plastic freezer bag; add chicken. Seal and chill 15 minutes, turning once. Remove chicken from marinade, discarding marinade.

3. Brush corn with 1 Tbsp. olive oil; sprinkle with remaining ½ tsp. salt.

4. Grill chicken and corn, covered with grill lid, 20 minutes, turning chicken once, and turning corn every 4 to 5 minutes. Remove chicken, and cover. Hold each grilled cob upright on a cutting board, and carefully cut downward, cutting kernels from cob.

5. Stir together cornbread mix and ⅔ cup water in a small bowl until smooth. Stir in basil and 1 cup grilled corn kernels. Pour about ¼ cup batter for each corncake onto a hot, lightly greased griddle. Cook cakes 3 to 4 minutes or until tops are covered with bubbles and edges look dry and cooked; turn and cook other side.

6. Thinly slice chicken. To serve, place 2 corncakes on each plate, top with chicken and 2 bacon slices.

7. Toss arugula with reserved lemon mixture. Place arugula mixture on bacon, and sprinkle with remaining corn kernels.

## Make It Easy:

**Use precooked bacon instead of cooking your own.**

# Pan-Grilled Chicken

## with Fresh Plum Salsa

MAKES **4 SERVINGS**
HANDS-ON **15 MIN.**
TOTAL **15 MIN.**

1 cup chopped ripe plums (about 2 plums)
1 small jalapeño pepper, seeded and diced
2 Tbsp. chopped fresh basil
2 Tbsp. chopped red onion
2 tsp. fresh lime juice
¾ tsp. salt, divided
2 Tbsp. brown sugar
½ tsp. ground cumin
4 (4-oz.) chicken breast cutlets
2 tsp. olive oil

*1.* Stir together plums, next 4 ingredients, and ¼ tsp. salt in a medium bowl.

*2.* Stir together brown sugar, cumin, and remaining ½ tsp. salt in a small bowl. Rub chicken with brown sugar mixture.

*3.* Cook chicken in hot oil in a grill pan or nonstick skillet over medium heat 3 minutes on each side or until done. Serve with plum mixture.

### Make It Easy:

**Thinly cut chicken cutlets cook faster than regular chicken breasts. If you don't have any on hand, you can pound thicker breasts yourself.**

# Basil-Peach Chicken
## with Quinoa

**MAKES 4 SERVINGS**
**HANDS-ON 30 MIN.**
**TOTAL 45 MIN.**

4 skinned and boned chicken breasts (about 2 lb.)
1 ¼ tsp. kosher salt
½ tsp. freshly ground black pepper
2 Tbsp. canola oil
1 shallot, thinly sliced
1 tsp. freshly grated ginger
2 garlic cloves, minced
12 fresh basil leaves, finely chopped
1 cup reduced-sodium fat-free chicken broth
4 large peaches, peeled and cut into ¼-inch-thick
     slices (about 2 cups)
Hot cooked quinoa
Garnish: fresh basil leaves

*1.* Preheat oven to 350°.

*2.* Season chicken on both sides with salt and pepper. Cook chicken in hot oil in a large ovenproof skillet over medium-high heat 2 minutes on each side or until browned. Remove chicken from skillet, reserving drippings in skillet.

*3.* Reduce heat to medium. Add shallot to hot drippings in skillet, and sauté 3 minutes or until tender. Add ginger and garlic; sauté 45 to 60 seconds or until fragrant. Add basil, chicken broth, and peaches. Return chicken to skillet, and turn to coat.

*4.* Bake at 350° for 15 minutes or until chicken is done. Serve over cooked quinoa, if desired.

## Kitchen Note:

*Starting the chicken on the stovetop and finishing it in the oven helps prevent dry, over-cooked chicken. The flavorful juices make a fresh and clean sauce—much lighter than a flour-thickened gravy.*

# Lemon Chicken

MAKES 8 SERVINGS
HANDS-ON 30 MIN.
TOTAL 30 MIN.

4 skinned and boned chicken breasts (about 1 ½ lb.)
1 tsp. salt
½ tsp. freshly ground black pepper
⅓ cup all-purpose flour
4 Tbsp. butter, divided
2 Tbsp. olive oil, divided
¼ cup chicken broth
¼ cup lemon juice
8 lemon slices
¼ cup chopped fresh flat-leaf parsley
Garnish: lemon slices

*1.* Cut each chicken breast in half lengthwise. Place chicken between 2 sheets of heavy-duty plastic wrap; flatten to ¼-inch thickness, using a rolling pin or flat side of a meat mallet. Sprinkle chicken with salt and pepper. Lightly dredge chicken in flour, shaking off excess.

*2.* Melt 1 Tbsp. butter with 1 Tbsp. olive oil in a large nonstick skillet over medium-high heat. Cook half of chicken in skillet 2 to 3 minutes on each side or until golden brown and done. Transfer chicken to a serving platter, and keep warm. Repeat procedure with 1 Tbsp. butter and remaining olive oil and chicken.

*3.* Add broth and lemon juice to skillet; cook 1 to 2 minutes or until sauce is slightly thickened, stirring to loosen particles from bottom of skillet. Add lemon slices.

*4.* Remove skillet from heat. Add parsley and remaining 2 Tbsp. butter; stir until butter melts. Pour sauce over chicken. Serve immediately.

## Kitchen Note:

*When purchasing parsley, look for bundles that are bright green without any wilting. To store it, wash and dry the parsley, then wrap it in a paper towel and place it in a bag in the refrigerator.*

## Simple Swap:

*You can also use amberjack, cobia, mahi-mahi, swordfish, mackerel, or salmon fillets in this dish.*

# Grilled Triggerfish
## with Potato Salad

**MAKES 4 SERVINGS**
**HANDS-ON 10 MIN.**
**TOTAL 10 MIN.**

Cooking spray
4 (6-oz.) triggerfish
2 Tbsp. extra virgin olive oil
½ tsp. table salt
¼ tsp. freshly ground black pepper
4 lemon slices or 1 tsp. lemon zest (optional)

*1.* Coat cold cooking grate of grill with cooking spray, and place on grill. Preheat grill to 400° (medium-high) heat.

*2.* Brush both sides of fish with olive oil; sprinkle with salt and pepper. Place fish on cooking grate, and grill, covered with grill lid, 4 minutes or until grill marks appear and fish no longer sticks to grate.

*3.* Using a metal spatula, carefully turn fish over, and grill, without grill lid, 2 minutes or just until fish flakes with a fork.

*4.* Serve with lemon slices or sprinkle with zest, if desired.

**SIMPLE POTATO SALAD**
**MAKES 4 TO 6 SERVINGS**
**HANDS-ON 15 MIN.**
**TOTAL 40 MIN.**

2 lb. small fingerling potatoes, halved lengthwise or quartered
2 tsp. kosher salt, divided
½ cup mayonnaise
1 Tbsp. red wine vinegar
1 Tbsp. whole grain mustard
2 tsp. chopped fresh flat-leaf parsley
1 tsp. freshly ground black pepper
1 garlic clove, minced
⅛ tsp. ground red pepper

*1.* Bring potatoes, 1 tsp. salt, and water to cover to a boil in a Dutch oven over medium-high heat. Reduce heat to medium-low, and cook, covered, 10 to 12 minutes or until potatoes are tender; drain. Place in a bowl; cool 15 minutes.

*2.* Meanwhile, stir together mayonnaise, next 6 ingredients, and remaining 1 tsp. salt in a small bowl.

*3.* Pour desired amount of dressing over potatoes; toss to coat. (Reserve any remaining dressing for another use.) Serve at room temperature.

# Classic Fried Catfish

MAKES **6 TO 8 SERVINGS**
HANDS-ON **20 MIN.**
TOTAL **8 HOURS, 30 MIN.**

1½ cups buttermilk
¼ tsp. hot sauce
6 (4- to 6-oz.) catfish fillets
⅓ cup plain yellow cornmeal
⅓ cup masa harina (corn flour)*
⅓ cup all-purpose flour
2 tsp. salt
1 tsp. freshly ground black pepper
1 tsp. ground red pepper
¼ tsp. garlic powder
Peanut oil
Garnish: lemon slices

*1.* Whisk together buttermilk and hot sauce. Place catfish in a single layer in a 13- x 9-inch baking dish; pour buttermilk mixture over fish. Cover and chill 8 hours, turning once.

*2.* Combine cornmeal and next 6 ingredients in a shallow dish.

*3.* Let fish stand at room temperature 10 minutes. Remove from buttermilk mixture, allowing excess to drip off. Dredge fish in cornmeal mixture, shaking off excess. Pour oil to depth of 2 inches into a large, deep cast-iron or heavy-duty skillet; heat to 360°.

*4.* Fry fish, in batches, 2 minutes on each side or until golden brown. Transfer to a wire rack on a paper towel-lined jelly-roll pan. Keep warm in a 225° oven until ready to serve. Serve with your favorite tartar sauce.

*All-purpose flour or plain yellow cornmeal may be substituted.

## Simple Swap:

*For an extra-crispy crust, use stone-ground yellow cornmeal. The secret to this recipe is maintaining an oil temperature of 360° for a crispy, golden crust.*

# Crunchy Crab Cakes

MAKES 8 SERVINGS
HANDS-ON 25 MIN.
TOTAL 25 MIN.

1 (16-oz.) package fresh lump crabmeat, drained
4 large lemons, divided
1 (4-oz.) jar diced pimiento, well drained
2 green onions, chopped
1 large egg, lightly beaten
2 Tbsp. mayonnaise
1 tsp. Old Bay seasoning
2 tsp. Dijon mustard
1 cup panko (Japanese breadcrumbs), divided
¼ cup canola oil
Garnishes: lemon zest, sliced green onions, sour
   cream

1. Pick crabmeat, removing any bits of shell.

2. Grate zest from 2 lemons to equal 2 tsp.; cut
   lemons in half, and squeeze juice to equal ¼ cup.
   Stir together lemon zest and juice, pimiento, and
   next 5 ingredients until well blended. Gently fold
   in crabmeat and ½ cup breadcrumbs.

3. Shape mixture into 8 patties. Dredge patties in
   remaining ½ cup breadcrumbs.

4. Cook half of patties in 2 Tbsp. hot oil in a large
   nonstick skillet over medium heat 2 minutes on
   each side or until golden brown; drain on a wire
   rack. Repeat procedure with remaining oil and
   patties.

5. Zest remaining 2 lemons.

## Kitchen Note:

*Serve these crab cakes over a salad for a delicious dinner. Or serve them on dinner rolls with lettuce, tomato, and a rémoulade sauce for a tasty slider.*

# Barbecue Shrimp

**MAKES 6 SERVINGS**
**HANDS-ON 10 MIN.**
**TOTAL 35 MIN.**

1½ lb. unpeeled jumbo raw shrimp
1 large lemon, cut into wedges
1 (0.7-oz.) envelope Italian dressing mix
½ cup melted butter
½ cup loosely packed fresh flat-leaf parsley

## Kitchen Note:

*Double the marinade for this recipe, because you'll want to use the leftover for dipping some crusty French bread.*

*1.* Preheat oven to 425°. Place shrimp and lemon in a 13- x 9-inch baking dish. Stir together dressing mix and butter. Pour butter mixture over shrimp, stirring to coat.

*2.* Bake, covered, at 425° for 25 to 30 minutes or just until shrimp turn pink, stirring once.

*3.* Remove shrimp mixture from oven, and sprinkle with parsley.

# Vegetable Gnocchi

## with Spinach-Herb Pesto

MAKES 4 SERVINGS
HANDS-ON 10 MIN.
TOTAL 45 MIN., INCLUDING PESTO

6 yellow squash (about 1 ¼ lb.)
8 sweet mini bell peppers
2 Tbsp. olive oil
1 tsp. salt
½ tsp. coarsely ground black pepper
1 (16-oz.) package gnocchi*
Spinach-Herb Pesto
½ (6-oz.) package baby spinach
¼ to ⅓ cup (1 to 1 ½ oz.) freshly shredded Parmesan cheese

*1.* Preheat oven to 425°.

*2.* Cut squash into 1-inch pieces. Cut bell peppers in half lengthwise; remove seeds. Stir together squash, bell peppers, oil, salt, and pepper. Arrange vegetables in a single layer on a jelly-roll pan, and bake at 425° for 15 minutes. Stir and bake 5 more minutes or until tender and golden.

*3.* Cook gnocchi according to package directions in a Dutch oven; drain. Return to Dutch oven. Add Spinach-Herb Pesto to gnocchi, and toss to coat. Add squash mixture and spinach, and gently toss to combine. Sprinkle with Parmesan cheese. Serve immediately.
*Medium-size pasta shells may be substituted.

Note: We tested with Gia Russa Gnocchi with Potato.

**SPINACH-HERB PESTO**
MAKES: ¾ CUP
HANDS-ON 15 MIN.
TOTAL 15 MIN.

½ (6-oz.) package baby spinach
1 Tbsp. chopped fresh cilantro
1 Tbsp. chopped fresh basil
1 tsp. lemon zest
2 Tbsp. lemon juice
1 tsp. chopped fresh mint
1 garlic clove, minced
¼ tsp. salt
½ cup (2 oz.) freshly shredded Parmesan cheese
¼ cup olive oil

Pulse first 8 ingredients in a food processor 6 to 7 times or until finely chopped. Add Parmesan cheese and oil; process until smooth, stopping to scrape down sides as needed. Use immediately, or store in refrigerator up to 48 hours. If chilled, let stand at room temperature 30 minutes before using; stir until blended.

## Kitchen Note:

**Substitute a store-bought pesto for this homemade one if you're short on time.**

# Fried Egg Sandwiches
## with Pancetta and Arugula

MAKES **4 SERVINGS**
HANDS-ON **25 MIN.**
TOTAL **25 MIN.**

4 (½-inch-thick) challah bread slices
2 Tbsp. butter, melted
1 (0.9-oz.) envelope hollandaise sauce mix
¼ tsp. lemon zest
1½ tsp. fresh lemon juice, divided
2 cups loosely packed arugula
½ cup loosely packed fresh flat-leaf parsley leaves
¼ cup thinly sliced red onion
3 tsp. extra virgin olive oil, divided
4 large eggs
¼ tsp. kosher salt
¼ tsp. freshly ground black pepper
12 thin pancetta slices, cooked
2 Tbsp. chopped sun-dried tomatoes

*1.* Preheat broiler with oven rack 5 to 6 inches from heat. Brush both sides of bread with butter; place on an aluminum foil-lined broiler pan. Broil 1 to 2 minutes on each side or until lightly toasted.

*2.* Prepare hollandaise sauce according to package directions; stir in zest and ½ tsp. lemon juice. Keep warm.

*3.* Toss together arugula, next 2 ingredients, 2 tsp. olive oil, and remaining 1 tsp. lemon juice.

*4.* Heat remaining 1 tsp. olive oil in a large nonstick skillet over medium heat. Gently break eggs into hot skillet; sprinkle with salt and pepper. Cook 2 to 3 minutes on each side or to desired degree of doneness.

*5.* Top bread slices with arugula mixture, pancetta slices, and fried eggs. Spoon hollandaise sauce over each egg, and sprinkle with tomatoes. Serve immediately.

## Simple Swap:

*Use brioche or thick sandwich bread in place of the challah.*

# Brown Sugar Waffles

MAKES 12 (4-INCH) WAFFLES
HANDS-ON 15 MIN.
TOTAL 25 MIN.

2 cups all-purpose flour
3 Tbsp. light brown sugar
1 tsp. baking powder
½ tsp. salt
¼ tsp. baking soda
2 large eggs
¾ cup buttermilk
¾ cup milk
⅓ cup unsalted butter, melted
Garnishes: butter, syrup, blueberries

1. Whisk together first 5 ingredients in a large bowl

2. Whisk together eggs and next 2 ingredients in a medium bowl. Add to flour mixture, and whisk just until blended. Whisk in melted butter.

3. Cook batter, in batches, in a preheated, oiled Belgian-style waffle iron until golden. (Cook times will vary.)

## Kitchen Note:

*Freeze any leftover waffles to liven up a weekday breakfast. They reheat nicely in the toaster.*

# Fried Okra Tacos

MAKES **4 SERVINGS**
HANDS-ON **10 MIN.**
TOTAL **55 MIN., INCLUDING OKRA AND SALSA**

**Tortillas**
**Shredded lettuce**
**Buttermilk Fried Okra**
**Fresh Tomato Salsa**
**Hot sauce**

Fill warm tortillas with shredded lettuce, hot Buttermilk Fried Okra, and Fresh Tomato Salsa. Serve with hot sauce.

## BUTTERMILK FRIED OKRA

MAKES **8 CUPS**
HANDS-ON **30 MIN.**
TOTAL **30 MIN.**

**1 lb. fresh okra, cut into ½-inch-thick slices**
**¾ cup buttermilk**
**1½ cups self-rising white cornmeal mix**
**1 tsp. salt**
**1 tsp. sugar**
**¼ tsp. ground red pepper**
**Vegetable oil**

*1.* Stir together okra and buttermilk in a large bowl. Stir together cornmeal mix and next 3 ingredients in a separate large bowl. Remove okra from buttermilk, in batches, using a slotted spoon, discarding buttermilk. Dredge in cornmeal mixture, and place in a wire-mesh strainer. Shake off excess.

*2.* Pour oil to depth of 1 inch into a large, deep cast-iron skillet or Dutch oven; heat to 375°. Fry okra, in batches, 4 minutes or until golden, turning once. Drain on paper towels.

## FRESH TOMATO SALSA

MAKES **ABOUT 5 CUPS**
HANDS-ON **15 MIN.**
TOTAL **15 MIN.**

**3 cups seeded and diced tomatoes (about 1½ lb.)**
**1 large avocado, diced**
**1 small green bell pepper, diced**
**½ cup chopped green onions**
**⅓ cup chopped fresh cilantro**
**1½ tsp. balsamic vinegar**
**½ tsp. seasoned salt**

Stir together diced tomatoes and next 6 ingredients. Season with salt to taste.

## Kitchen Note:

*If you're in a rush, purchase fried okra from the grocery store deli and fresh salsa from the produce section for a super-fast weeknight meal.*

# Skillet Kale Pizza

MAKES 4 SERVINGS
HANDS-ON 20 MIN.
TOTAL 1 HOUR, 32 MIN.

1 lb. bakery pizza dough
Vegetable cooking spray
½ cup sliced red onion
1 garlic clove, sliced
2 Tbsp. olive oil, divided
4 cups firmly packed coarsely chopped kale
1 tsp. chopped fresh rosemary
1 Tbsp. red wine vinegar
2 tsp. plain yellow cornmeal
½ cup crumbled blue cheese
½ cup (2 oz.) shredded fontina cheese
¼ tsp. dried crushed red pepper

1. Place dough in a large bowl coated with cooking spray; lightly coat dough with cooking spray. Cover with a clean cloth, and let rise in a warm place (85°), free from drafts, 1 hour.

2. Roll dough to a 14-inch circle on a lightly floured surface; cover with plastic wrap.

3. Preheat oven to 450°. Cook onion and garlic in 1 Tbsp. hot oil in a 12-inch cast-iron skillet over medium-high heat, stirring often, 2 minutes or until onion is tender. Add kale and rosemary. Cook, stirring constantly, 2 minutes or just until wilted. Stir in vinegar. Add salt to taste. Transfer to a bowl.

4. Wipe skillet clean. Reduce heat to medium. Coat skillet with 2 tsp. oil; sprinkle with cornmeal. Arrange dough in skillet, gently stretching edges to cover bottom and sides of skillet. Cook over medium heat 2 minutes. Remove from heat. Top with kale mixture and cheeses. Brush edges with remaining 1 tsp. oil.

5. Bake at 450° for 12 to 15 minutes or until crust is golden. Sprinkle with red pepper.

## Make It Easy:

*Use prepackaged kale. It's a big time-saver in this recipe.*

# Cheese Ravioli

## with Tomatoes and Mascarpone

MAKES 6 SERVINGS
HANDS-ON 15 MIN.
TOTAL 20 MIN.

- 1 (24-oz.) package frozen cheese-filled ravioli
- 3 pt. assorted grape tomatoes
- 1 large tomato, chopped
- 2 garlic cloves, chopped
- 2 Tbsp. olive oil
- ¼ cup butter, cubed
- 1 Tbsp. fresh lemon juice
- ¾ tsp. kosher salt
- ¼ tsp. freshly ground black pepper
- ½ cup torn assorted fresh herbs (such as parsley and basil)
- 1 (8-oz.) container mascarpone cheese

*1.* Prepare pasta according to package directions.

*2.* Meanwhile, preheat broiler with oven rack 4 to 5 inches from heat. Stir together tomatoes, garlic, and olive oil in a 15- x 10-inch jelly-roll pan. Broil 5 to 8 minutes or until tomatoes are charred, stirring halfway through.

*3.* Transfer tomato mixture to a large bowl. Stir in butter, next 3 ingredients, and ¼ cup fresh herbs. Spoon over hot cooked ravioli; dollop with cheese. Sprinkle with remaining ¼ cup fresh herbs. Serve immediately.

Note: We tested with Celentano Cheese Ravioli.

## Kitchen Note:

*Blister and burst tomatoes under the broiler to concentrate flavor. Use extras to fill omelets or sandwiches.*

# Slow-Cooked Meals to Savor

**Make It Easy:**

Use a slow-cooker liner to make cleanup a breeze.

# Braised Short Ribs

## with Vegetables

MAKES 8 SERVINGS
HANDS-ON 15 MIN.
TOTAL 6 HOURS, 35 MIN.

4 lb. beef short ribs, trimmed and cut in half
1½ tsp. salt
½ tsp. freshly ground black pepper
1 Tbsp. vegetable oil
1 (14-oz.) can fat-free beef broth
1 (14½-oz.) can diced tomatoes, drained
½ cup dry red wine
4 carrots, peeled and coarsely chopped
1 medium-size sweet onion, cut into 8 wedges
1 tsp. dried thyme
Garnish: chopped fresh thyme

1. Rinse short ribs, and pat dry. Remove and discard silver skin, if necessary. Sprinkle ribs with salt and pepper.

2. Cook short ribs in hot oil in a Dutch oven over medium heat 10 minutes on each side or until browned. Transfer ribs to a 6-qt. slow cooker.

3. Add broth and next 5 ingredients to slow cooker. Cover and cook on HIGH 6 hours or until meat is tender. Serve over grits.

## Great Grits

Grits can vary depending on whether they're ground at a gristmill or purchased at the supermarket.

**HOMINY:** Dried white or yellow corn kernels from which the hull and germ are removed. It's sold dried or ready-to-eat in cans. When dried hominy is ground, it's called hominy grits.

**WHOLE-GROUND:** These grits are coarse ground. They can be found at specialty food stores.

**QUICK AND REGULAR GRITS:** Quick grits are ground fine and cook in 5 minutes; regular grits are a medium grind and cook in 10 minutes.

# Italian Pot Roast

MAKES 6 SERVINGS
HANDS-ON 20 MIN.
TOTAL 9 HOURS

8-oz. sliced fresh mushrooms
1 large sweet onion, cut in half and sliced
1 (3- to 4-lb.) boneless chuck roast, trimmed
1 tsp. black pepper
2 Tbsp. olive oil
1 (1-oz.) envelope dry onion soup mix
1 (14-oz.) can beef broth
1 (8-oz.) can tomato sauce
3 Tbsp. tomato paste
1 tsp. dried Italian seasoning
2 Tbsp. cornstarch
1 (8.8-oz.) package pappardelle pasta
Garnish: fresh basil leaves

1. Place mushrooms and onion in a lightly greased 5- to 6-qt. slow cooker.

2. Sprinkle roast with pepper. Cook roast in hot oil in a large skillet over medium-high heat 2 to 3 minutes on each side or until browned.

3. Place roast on top of mushrooms and onion in slow cooker. Sprinkle onion soup mix over roast; pour beef broth and tomato sauce over roast. Cover and cook on LOW 8 to 10 hours or until meat shreds easily with a fork.

4. Transfer roast to a cutting board; cut into large chunks, removing any large pieces of fat. Keep roast warm.

5. Skim fat from juices in slow cooker; stir in tomato paste and Italian seasoning. Stir together cornstarch and 2 Tbsp. water in a small bowl until smooth; add to juices in slow cooker, stirring until blended. Increase slow cooker heat to HIGH. Cover and cook 40 minutes or until mixture is thickened. Add roast.

6. Cook pappardelle according to package directions. Serve roast over pappardelle.

## Make It Easy:

**Brown the beef the night before and store in the refrigerator overnight. It saves a step when preparing the recipe for the slow cooker the next morning.**

# Barbecued Brisket
## with Lone-Star Slaw

MAKES 4 TO 6 SERVINGS
HANDS-ON 20 MIN.
TOTAL 7 HOURS, 40 MIN.

1 large sweet onion, sliced
3 garlic cloves, chopped
1 Tbsp. chili powder
1 Tbsp. jarred beef soup base
1 Tbsp. Worcestershire sauce
1 tsp. ground cumin
½ tsp. freshly ground black pepper
1½ tsp. hickory liquid smoke
1 (2- to 3-lb.) beef brisket flat, trimmed
¼ cup beer
3 Tbsp. bottled chili sauce

1. Lightly grease a 6-qt. slow cooker; add onion and garlic. Stir together chili powder and next 5 ingredients. Rub over brisket; place brisket over onion mixture in slow cooker.

2. Whisk together beer and chili sauce. Slowly pour mixture around brisket (to avoid removing spices from brisket).

3. Cover and cook on LOW 7 to 8 hours (or on HIGH 4 to 5 hours) or until meat is fork-tender. Uncover and let stand in slow cooker 20 minutes.

4. Remove brisket from slow cooker; cut brisket across the grain into thin slices. Return brisket to slow cooker, and spoon pan juices over meat.

Note: We tested with Heinz Chili Sauce.

LONE STAR SLAW
MAKES 4 TO 6 SERVINGS
HANDS-ON 20 MIN.
TOTAL 20 MIN.

¼ cup apple cider vinegar
¼ cup canola oil
2 Tbsp. mayonnaise
1 Tbsp. honey
½ tsp. salt
¼ tsp. freshly ground black pepper
¼ tsp. celery seeds
1 (16-oz.) package shredded coleslaw mix
½ tsp. grapefruit zest
2 Tbsp. fresh grapefruit juice
1 grapefruit, sectioned
¾ cup toasted chopped pecans
1 Tbsp. chopped fresh cilantro

Whisk together vinegar, canola oil, mayonnaise, honey, salt, pepper, and celery seeds in a large bowl. Stir in coleslaw mix, grapefruit zest, grapefruit juice, grapefruit sections, toasted pecans, and chopped fresh cilantro. Serve immediately, or chill up to 24 hours.

# Beef Nachos

MAKES 6 SERVINGS
HANDS-ON 20 MIN.
TOTAL 8 HOURS, 30 MIN.

1 (3-lb.) boneless beef rump roast
1 Tbsp. vegetable oil
1 (12-oz.) jar mild banana pepper rings
1 (14-oz.) can beef broth
3 garlic cloves, minced
Tortilla chips
1 (15-oz.) can black beans, rinsed
Tomatoes, chopped
Onion, finely chopped
Shredded Monterey Jack cheese
Cilantro, avocado, and sour cream

1. Season roast with salt and pepper to taste. Brown all sides of roast in hot oil in a large skillet over high heat.

2. Place roast in a 6-qt. slow cooker. Add banana pepper rings, beef broth, and garlic. Cover and cook on LOW 8 hours or until meat shreds easily. Transfer to a cutting board, reserving liquid in slow cooker. Shred roast; return to slow cooker. Keep warm on LOW.

3. Preheat oven to 350°. Place tortilla chips on a baking sheet; top with shredded beef, black beans, tomatoes, onion, and cheese. Bake 10 minutes. Serve with cilantro, avocado, and sour cream.

## Make It Easy:

*Use jarred minced garlic in place of mincing the garlic cloves.*

# Spiced Beef Stew

## with Sweet Potatoes

MAKES 8 SERVINGS
HANDS-ON 50 MIN.
TOTAL 6 HOURS, 50 MIN.

1 (6-oz.) can tomato paste
1 (32-oz.) container beef broth
1 (3-lb.) boneless chuck roast, trimmed and cut into
    1½-inch cubes
3 Tbsp. all-purpose flour
1½ tsp. salt
1 tsp. freshly ground black pepper
2 Tbsp. olive oil
2 lb. small sweet potatoes, peeled and cubed
2 sweet onions, cut into eighths
2 cups cubed butternut squash (about 1 lb.)
2 cups frozen whole kernel corn, thawed
2 celery ribs, sliced
4 garlic cloves, minced
2 tsp. ancho chile powder
1 tsp. smoked paprika
1 tsp. dried thyme

*1.* Whisk together first 2 ingredients until smooth.

*2.* Sprinkle beef with flour, salt, and pepper; toss to coat.

*3.* Cook beef, in batches, in hot oil in a large skillet over medium-high heat, stirring occasionally, 10 to 12 minutes or until browned. Place in a 6-qt. slow cooker. Add sweet potatoes, next 8 ingredients, and broth mixture. Cover and cook on HIGH 6 to 7 hours or until tender.

## Make It Easy:

**Purchase cubed butternut squash from the produce section of the grocery store.**

# Spicy Chili

## with Beef and Black Beans

MAKES 8 SERVINGS
HANDS-ON 19 MIN.
TOTAL 8 HOURS, 19 MIN.

2 lb. boneless top sirloin steak, cubed*
2 Tbsp. vegetable oil
3 (15.5-oz.) cans black beans
2 (14.5-oz.) cans diced tomatoes
2 (4.5-oz.) cans chopped green chiles
1 large sweet onion, diced
1 green bell pepper, diced
4 garlic cloves, minced
1 (12-oz.) can beer
1 (3.625-oz.) package chili seasoning kit
Toppings: shredded Cheddar cheese, diced tomatoes and avocado, sour cream, sliced green onions, chopped fresh cilantro

1. Sauté steak in hot oil in a large skillet over medium-high heat 4 to 5 minutes or until browned.

2. Place steak in a lightly greased 6-qt. slow cooker; stir in black beans and next 6 ingredients. Stir in packets from chili kit, omitting masa and red pepper packets. Cover and cook on LOW 8 hours. Serve with desired toppings.

*2 lb. ground round may be substituted. Omit oil. Brown ground round in a large skillet over medium-high heat, stirring often, 8 minutes or until meat crumbles and is no longer pink; drain. Proceed with recipe as directed. Hands-on 23 min. Total 8 hours, 23 min.

Note: We tested with Wick Fowler's 2-Alarm Chili Kit at one tasting and with 1 (4-oz.) package Carroll Shelby's Original Texas Brand Chili Kit at another.

## Kitchen Note:

*Serve this chili with cornbread waffles for a complete one-dish meal. Prepare batter from 2 (6-oz.) packages buttermilk cornbread mix according to package directions. Cook batter, in batches, in a preheated, oiled waffle iron until done.*

# Wine-Braised Oxtails

MAKES ABOUT 6 SERVINGS
HANDS-ON 30 MIN.
TOTAL 6 HOURS, 30 MIN.

2 carrots, chopped
2 medium onions, chopped
2 celery ribs, chopped
6 garlic cloves, sliced
6 fresh flat-leaf parsley sprigs
2 bay leaves
2 (3-inch) fresh rosemary sprigs
5 lb. oxtails
2 tsp. kosher salt
1 tsp. freshly ground black pepper
¼ cup all-purpose flour
2 Tbsp. olive oil
2 cups dry red wine
1 (6-oz.) can tomato paste
1 (8-oz.) package fresh mushrooms, quartered
Hot cooked rice

*1.* Place first 7 ingredients in a 6-qt. slow cooker.

*2.* Toss oxtails with salt and pepper. Sprinkle with flour; toss to coat. Cook oxtails, in 2 batches, in hot oil in a large skillet over medium heat 3 to 4 minutes on each side or until well browned. Transfer oxtails to slow cooker, reserving drippings in skillet.

*3.* Add wine to reserved drippings in skillet; cook 1 minute, stirring to loosen brown bits from bottom of skillet. Whisk in tomato paste; cook, stirring often, 2 minutes. Pour over oxtails.

*4.* Cover and cook on LOW 5 to 6 hours. Add mushrooms; cook 1 more hour.

*5.* Remove oxtails and vegetables using a slotted spoon. Discard bay leaves and herbs. Skim fat from juices in slow cooker; season with salt and pepper. Serve immediately over oxtails, vegetables, and hot cooked rice.

## Simple Swap:

*You can use short ribs in place of oxtails in this recipe. Both cook well with a long, slow braising.*

# Chile Verde
## with Green Tomatoes

MAKES 8 SERVINGS
HANDS-ON 30 MIN.
TOTAL 6 HOURS, 45 MIN., INCLUDING SALSA

6 medium-size green tomatoes, divided
4 poblano peppers, seeded and divided
1½ cups chopped fresh cilantro
5 garlic cloves
½ cup chopped sweet onion
½ cup hot water
1 (5-lb.) boneless pork shoulder roast (Boston butt)
2 tsp. ground cumin
1 tsp. salt
1 tsp. black pepper
¼ cup all-purpose flour
¼ cup olive oil
Corn tortillas, warmed
Green Tomato Salsa

1. Chop 3 tomatoes and 1 poblano pepper, and place in a large bowl. Stir in cilantro and next 3 ingredients. Process mixture, in 2 batches, in a blender or food processor until smooth.

2. Coarsely chop remaining tomatoes and peppers, and place in a 6-qt. slow cooker.

3. Trim and discard fat from pork. Cut pork into 2-inch cubes. Combine pork and next 3 ingredients in a large bowl, and toss to coat. Sprinkle with flour, and toss to coat.

4. Cook pork, in batches, in hot oil in a large skillet over medium-high heat, turning occasionally, 10 to 12 minutes or until golden brown. Place pork over tomato mixture in slow cooker. Pour pureed tomato mixture over pork.

5. Cover and cook on LOW 6 to 7 hours or until pork is tender. Season with salt and pepper. Serve chile verde with tortillas and Green Tomato Salsa.

**GREEN TOMATO SALSA**
MAKES 2 CUPS
HANDS-ON 15 MIN.
TOTAL 15 MIN.

Combine 2 medium-size green tomatoes, finely chopped; ½ small onion, finely chopped; 1 jalapeño pepper, seeded and minced; ½ cup chopped fresh cilantro; 1 Tbsp. fresh lime juice; and ½ tsp. salt in a bowl. Cover and chill until ready to serve.

## Kitchen Note:

**You can use green tomato salsa from the refrigerator section of the grocery store as a quick substitute for making your own.**

# Easy Brunswick Stew

MAKES: 8 SERVINGS
HANDS-ON 15 MIN.
TOTAL 10 HOURS, 15 MIN.

3 lb. boneless pork shoulder roast (Boston butt)
2 medium-size new potatoes, peeled and chopped
1 large onion, chopped
1 (28-oz.) can crushed tomatoes
1 (18-oz.) bottle barbecue sauce
1 (14-oz.) can chicken broth
1 (9-oz.) package frozen baby lima beans, thawed
1 (10-oz.) package frozen corn, thawed
6 Tbsp. brown sugar
1 tsp. salt

*1.* Trim roast, and cut into 2-inch pieces. Stir together all ingredients in a 6-qt. slow cooker.

*2.* Cover and cook on LOW 10 hours or until potatoes are fork-tender. Remove pork with a slotted spoon, and shred with two forks. Return shredded pork to slow cooker, and stir well. Ladle stew into bowls.

## Kitchen Note:

*Cooking the stew on low heat for a long time makes the meat extremely tender and easy to shred. High heat yields a less tender product.*

# Barbecue Ribs

## with Orange Glaze

**MAKES 6 SERVINGS**
**HANDS-ON 11 MIN.**
**TOTAL 8 HOURS, 32 MIN.**

Cooking spray
2 slabs pork baby back ribs (about 5 lb.), cut in half
1 cup barbecue sauce
¼ cup molasses
¼ cup frozen orange juice concentrate, thawed
2 tsp. hot sauce
1 tsp. jarred minced garlic
¼ tsp. salt
Garnish: orange slices

### Kitchen Note:

**Brown the ribs before putting them in the slow cooker to bring out the flavor in the meat.**

1. Preheat broiler with oven rack 5 ½ inches from heat. Coat the rack of a broiler pan and broiler pan with cooking spray. Place ribs on rack in broiler pan. Broil 10 minutes.

2. Meanwhile, stir together barbecue sauce and next 5 ingredients in a medium bowl.

3. Arrange ribs in a 6-qt. oval slow cooker. Pour sauce over ribs.

4. Cover and cook on LOW 8 hours. Transfer ribs to a serving platter. Skim fat from juices in slow cooker. Pour juices into a 2-qt. saucepan. Cook over medium-high heat 10 minutes or until reduced to 1 ½ cups, stirring occasionally. Serve sauce with ribs.

# Roast Pork Loin

## with Apples and Bacon

MAKES 6 TO 8 SERVINGS
HANDS-ON 50 MIN.
TOTAL 3 HOURS, 50 MIN.

1 (3-lb.) boneless pork loin
½ tsp. kosher salt
½ tsp. freshly ground black pepper
6 oz. thinly sliced pancetta or bacon
Kitchen string
2 Tbsp. olive oil
2 small onions, quartered (root end intact)
1 (12-oz.) package frozen pearl onions (about 2 cups)
2 garlic cloves, thinly sliced
3 fresh thyme sprigs
2 bay leaves
1 (12-oz.) bottle stout or porter beer
2 Tbsp. Dijon mustard
3 firm apples (such as Gala), divided
2 cups jarred sauerkraut, rinsed
2 cups finely shredded green cabbage
1 Tbsp. chopped fresh flat-leaf parsley
1 tsp. fresh lemon juice
½ cup apricot preserves
¼ cup chicken broth

1. Trim fat and silver skin from pork. Sprinkle pork with kosher salt and pepper. Wrap top and sides of pork with pancetta. Tie with kitchen string, securing at 1-inch intervals.

2. Cook pork in hot oil in a large skillet over medium heat, turning occasionally, 15 minutes or until deep golden brown. Remove from skillet, reserving drippings in skillet.

3. Place quartered onion and next 4 ingredients in a 6-qt. slow cooker; top with pork.

4. Add beer to reserved drippings in skillet, and cook over medium heat 8 minutes or until liquid is reduced by half, stirring to loosen browned bits from bottom of skillet. Stir in mustard, and pour over pork. Cover and cook on HIGH 2 hours.

5. Peel 2 apples, and cut into large wedges. Add apple wedges, sauerkraut, and cabbage to slow cooker; cover and cook 1 to 2 more hours or until a meat thermometer inserted into thickest portion of pork registers 150° and apples are tender.

6. Cut remaining unpeeled apple into thin strips, and toss with parsley and lemon juice. Season with salt and pepper to taste.

7. Combine preserves and broth in a small saucepan, and cook over medium heat, stirring often, 4 to 5 minutes or until melted and smooth.

8. Brush pork with apricot mixture. Cut pork into slices, and serve with onion mixture, apple-parsley mixture, and additional Dijon mustard.

# King Ranch Chicken

MAKES 6 SERVINGS
HANDS-ON 10 MIN.
TOTAL 4 HOURS, 10 MIN.

4 cups chopped cooked chicken
1 large onion, chopped
1 large green bell pepper, chopped
1 (10 ¾-oz.) can cream of chicken soup
1 (10 ¾-oz.) can cream of mushroom soup
1 (10-oz.) can diced tomatoes and green chiles
1 garlic clove, minced
1 tsp. chili powder
12 (6-inch) fajita-size corn tortillas
2 cups (8 oz.) shredded sharp Cheddar cheese

1. Stir together first 8 ingredients. Tear tortillas into 1-inch pieces; layer one-third of tortilla pieces in a lightly greased 6-qt. slow cooker. Top with one-third of chicken mixture and ⅔ cup cheese. Repeat layers twice.

2. Cover and cook on LOW 3 ½ hours or until bubbly and edges are golden brown. Uncover and cook on LOW 30 minutes.

## Kitchen Note:

*Remove the slow cooker's lid during the last 30 minutes of cooking to give this an oven-baked flavor and texture.*

# Chicken Stew
## with Dumplings

**MAKES 8 SERVINGS**
**HANDS-ON 30 MIN.**
**TOTAL 5 HOURS, 40 MIN.**

### CHICKEN
- 3 skinned, bone-in chicken breasts (about 1 ½ lb.)
- 6 skinned and boned chicken thighs (about 1 lb.)
- 1 tsp. salt
- ½ tsp. freshly ground black pepper
- ½ tsp. poultry seasoning
- ½ lb. carrots, sliced
- ½ lb. parsnips, sliced
- 4 celery ribs, sliced
- 1 sweet onion, chopped
- 2 (10 ¾-oz.) cans cream of chicken soup
- 1 (32-oz.) container chicken broth

### CORNBREAD DUMPLINGS
- 1 ½ cups all-purpose flour
- ½ cup self-rising yellow cornmeal
- 2 tsp. baking powder
- ½ tsp. salt
- 1 cup milk
- 3 Tbsp. butter, melted
- ¼ tsp. dried thyme
- 2 tsp. chopped fresh flat-leaf parsley

1. Prepare Chicken: Rub chicken pieces with salt, pepper, and poultry seasoning. Place breasts in a 6-qt. slow cooker, top with thighs. Add carrots and next 3 ingredients. Whisk together soup and broth until smooth. Pour soup mixture over vegetables. Cover and cook on HIGH 3 ½ hours or until chicken shreds easily with a fork. Remove chicken; cool 10 minutes. Bone and shred chicken. Stir chicken into soup-and-vegetable mixture. Cover and cook on HIGH 1 hour or until boiling.

2. Meanwhile, prepare Dumplings: Whisk together flour and next 3 ingredients. Make a well in center of mixture. Add milk, butter, thyme, and parsley to dry ingredients, gently stirring just until moistened.

3. Drop dough by ¼ cupfuls into simmering chicken mixture, leaving about ¼-inch space between dumplings. Cover and cook on HIGH 30 to 35 minutes or until dumplings have doubled in size.

### Kitchen Note:

**Be sure to use a 6-quart slow cooker to prepare this recipe. The chicken and dumplings need lots of room to cook.**

# Chicken Marsala

MAKES 8 SERVINGS
HANDS-ON 20 MIN.
TOTAL 5 HOURS, 35 MIN.

2 garlic cloves, finely chopped
1 Tbsp. vegetable oil
8 skinned and boned chicken breasts
½ tsp. salt
½ tsp. black pepper
2 (6-oz.) jars sliced mushrooms, drained
1 cup sweet Marsala wine or chicken broth
¼ cup cornstarch
Hot cooked rice
Garnish: chopped fresh parsley

1. Combine garlic and oil in a lightly greased 4- or 5-qt. slow cooker. Sprinkle chicken with salt and pepper; place in slow cooker. Arrange mushrooms over chicken, and pour in wine.

2. Cover and cook on LOW 5 to 6 hours. Remove chicken from slow cooker; cover to keep warm.

3. Stir together ½ cup water and cornstarch until smooth; stir cornstarch mixture into liquid in slow cooker. Increase heat to HIGH. Cover and cook 10 minutes or until sauce is slightly thickened.

4. Return chicken to slow cooker. Cover and cook on HIGH 5 minutes or until hot. Serve over hot cooked rice.

## Kitchen Note:

**Top this dish with toasted pecans for extra flavor.**

# Barbecued Drumettes
## with Spicy Asian Glaze

**MAKES 2 TO 4 SERVINGS**
**HANDS-ON 15 MIN.**
**TOTAL 3 HOURS, 15 MIN.**

3 lb. chicken drumettes (about 20)
½ tsp. salt
¼ tsp. black pepper
1 cup honey-barbecue sauce
1 Tbsp. Asian hot chili sauce (such as Sriracha)
1 Tbsp. soy sauce
3 garlic cloves, pressed
Garnishes: toasted sesame seeds, sliced green
    onions (optional)

*1.* Preheat broiler with oven rack 3 inches from heat.

*2.* Sprinkle drumettes with salt and pepper. Place on a lightly greased rack in a broiler pan. Broil 8 minutes or until browned. Place drumettes in a lightly greased 4-qt. slow cooker.

*3.* Combine barbecue sauce and next 3 ingredients; pour over drumettes. Cover and cook on LOW 3 hours. Serve with sauce from slow cooker for dipping.

## Kitchen Note:

*Look for Asian hot chili sauce with Asian foods on the grocery shelves. It's a staple in parts of Asia—much like ketchup is in the States. It's an easy way to add a spicy flavor to this dish.*

# Creole Chicken
## with Field Pea Succotash

**MAKES 6 SERVINGS**
**HANDS-ON 10 MIN.**
**TOTAL 5 HOURS, 10 MIN.**

1 (16-oz.) package frozen field peas with snaps, thawed
1 (10-oz.) package frozen vegetable gumbo mix, thawed
1 (16-oz.) package frozen baby gold and white whole kernel corn, thawed
2 tsp. chicken bouillon granules
4 tsp. Creole seasoning, divided
1½ tsp. paprika
6 skinned, bone-in chicken thighs (about 2½ lb.)
2 Tbsp. canola oil

*1.* Mix together first 4 ingredients and 2 tsp. Creole seasoning in a lightly greased 6-qt. oval-shaped slow cooker.

*2.* Combine paprika and remaining 2 tsp. Creole seasoning; rub over chicken. Heat oil in a large skillet over medium-high heat; add chicken to pan, and cook 4 minutes on each side or until browned. Arrange chicken on top of vegetable mixture. Cover and cook on LOW 5 to 6 hours or until chicken is done.

Note: We tested with PictSweet Field Peas with Snaps, PictSweet Gumbo Vegetables, and Birds Eye Baby Gold & White Corn.

## Make It Easy:

*Use a sharp knife to quickly remove the skin from the chicken thighs. If your hands keep slipping, then use a paper towel to grip the chicken.*

# Slow Cooker Chicken
## with Rosemary Potatoes

MAKES 6 TO 8 SERVINGS
HANDS-ON 25 MIN.
TOTAL 4 HOURS, 25 MIN.

3 carrots or celery ribs
5 lb. chicken leg quarters
2 Tbsp. chopped fresh rosemary
2 tsp. pimentón (sweet smoked Spanish paprika)
2 ½ tsp. kosher salt, divided
1 ¼ tsp. freshly ground black pepper, divided
12 garlic cloves, sliced
3 Tbsp. olive oil
½ cup chicken broth
2 lb. fingerling Yukon gold potatoes, halved
1 tsp. olive oil
Garnish: fresh rosemary

1. Place carrots in a single layer in a 5-qt. slow cooker.

2. Remove skin from chicken, and trim fat. Stir together rosemary, pimentón, 1 ½ tsp. salt, and 1 tsp. pepper. Rub mixture over chicken.

3. Sauté garlic in 3 Tbsp. hot oil in a large skillet over medium heat 2 minutes or until golden brown. Transfer to a bowl using a slotted spoon; reserve oil in skillet. Cook half of chicken in reserved oil in skillet 3 to 4 minutes on each side or until deep golden brown. Transfer to slow cooker, reserving drippings in skillet. Repeat with remaining chicken.

4. Add broth and garlic to reserved drippings in skillet, and cook 1 minute, stirring to loosen particles from bottom of skillet; pour over chicken in slow cooker. Cover and cook on HIGH 2 hours.

5. Toss potatoes with 1 tsp. oil and remaining 1 tsp. salt and ¼ tsp. pepper; add to slow cooker. Cover and cook 2 more hours.

6. Transfer chicken and potatoes to a serving platter, and pour juices from slow cooker through a fine wire-mesh strainer into a bowl; skim fat from juices. Serve immediately with chicken and potatoes.

## Make It Easy:

*You can swap baby red or new potatoes for the Yukon gold potatoes in this recipe.*

# Creole Gumbo
## with Shrimp and Sausage

MAKES 6 SERVINGS
HANDS-ON 35 MIN.
TOTAL 6 HOURS, 25 MIN.

½ cup all-purpose flour
1 lb. andouille sausage, sliced
1 (14 ½-oz.) can diced tomatoes
1 large onion, chopped
1 large green bell pepper, chopped
2 celery ribs, chopped
4 garlic cloves, chopped
3 bay leaves
2 tsp. Creole seasoning
½ tsp. dried thyme
4 cups chicken broth
3 lb. unpeeled, large raw shrimp, peeled and
     deveined
1 bunch green onions, sliced
¼ cup chopped fresh flat-leaf parsley
Garnish: sliced green onions

*1.* Preheat oven to 400°. Sprinkle flour in a 9-inch cast-iron skillet. Bake 10 to 15 minutes or until golden brown, stirring once. Cool 10 minutes.

*2.* Meanwhile, cook sausage in a Dutch oven over medium heat, stirring occasionally, 5 minutes or until browned. Drain on paper towels. Place sausage in a 6-qt. slow cooker; add tomatoes and next 7 ingredients.

*3.* Whisk together browned flour and broth until smooth. Pour into slow cooker. Cover and cook on HIGH 5 to 6 hours. Stir in shrimp, green onions, and parsley. Cover and cook on HIGH 30 minutes, stirring once. Discard bay leaves before serving.

## Kitchen Note:

*For a quick supper, serve this with herbed rice. Stir together 3 cups hot cooked rice and ¼ cup chopped fresh flat-leaf parsley.*

# No-Cook Wonders

# Peach Gazpacho
## with Cucumber Yogurt

MAKES ABOUT 5 CUPS
HANDS-ON 20 MIN.
TOTAL 1 HOUR, 20 MIN.

5 large peaches, peeled and divided
3 large tomatoes, cored and divided
½ medium-size sweet onion, coarsely chopped
    (about ½ cup)
3 Tbsp. apple cider vinegar
Kosher salt and freshly ground white pepper
¾ cup finely diced English cucumber
⅓ cup plain Greek yogurt
2 Tbsp. chopped fresh chives
1 garlic clove, minced
Extra virgin olive oil
Garnish: fresh chive pieces

1. Quarter 4 peaches and 2 tomatoes. Process quartered peaches and tomatoes and next 2 ingredients in a food processor until smooth.

2. Chop remaining peach and tomato. Stir into pureed mixture. Season with kosher salt and freshly ground white pepper to taste. Cover and chill 1 hour.

3. Meanwhile, combine cucumber and next 3 ingredients in a medium bowl. Season with kosher salt and freshly ground white pepper to taste. Cover and chill 1 to 24 hours. (Chilling can dull the seasoning, so you may need to add more salt and pepper before serving.)

4. Ladle gazpacho into bowls. Spoon cucumber mixture over gazpacho. Drizzle each serving with about 1 tsp. extra virgin olive oil. Serve soup immediately.

## Make It Easy:

*Blanch the peaches before you peel them to loosen the skin and make it easier to remove.*

# Turkey Sandwich

## with Bacon and Havarti

**MAKES 4 SERVINGS**
**HANDS-ON 20 MIN.**
**TOTAL 1 HOUR, 20 MIN.**

1 (7-inch) round sourdough bread loaf
¼ cup balsamic vinaigrette
½ lb. thinly sliced smoked deli turkey
1 (12-oz.) jar roasted red bell peppers,
    drained and sliced
6 (1-oz.) slices Havarti cheese
4 fully cooked bacon slices

*1.* Cut top 2 inches off sourdough loaf, reserving top; hollow out loaf, leaving a 1-inch-thick shell. (Reserve soft center of bread loaf for another use.)

*2.* Drizzle 2 Tbsp. vinaigrette evenly in bottom bread shell; layer with half of turkey, peppers, and cheese. Repeat layers, and top with bacon. Drizzle evenly with remaining 2 Tbsp. vinaigrette, and cover with reserved bread top; press down firmly. Wrap in plastic wrap, and chill at least 1 hour or up to 8 hours before serving. Cut into 4 wedges.

### Kitchen Note:

*A semisoft Danish cheese with small irregular holes, Havarti cheese boasts a mild flavor. You can also serve Swiss or Muenster on this sandwich.*

# Turkey Wraps

## with Cranberry Goat Cheese

MAKES 3 DOZEN
HANDS-ON 30 MIN.
TOTAL 30 MIN.

1 (8-oz.) package cream cheese, softened
2 (4-oz.) packages goat cheese, softened
¾ cup sweetened dried cranberries, coarsely
    chopped
¼ cup chopped toasted walnuts
2 tsp. honey
1 garlic clove, minced
½ tsp. chopped fresh rosemary
¼ tsp. black pepper
8 (10-inch) flour tortillas
1 lb. thinly sliced turkey
4 cups fresh baby spinach

1. Stir together cream cheese, goat cheese, cranberries, walnuts, honey, minced garlic, rosemary, and pepper. Season with salt to taste. Cover and chill up to 3 days.

2. Spread 2 Tbsp. cream cheese mixture onto each tortilla, leaving a ½-inch border around edges. Divide turkey and spinach among tortillas. Roll up, and cut in half or into slices.

## Make It Easy:

**Make the cream cheese mixture ahead to speed up the sandwich prep.**

# Dagwood Sandwiches

MAKES 4 SANDWICHES
HANDS-ON 17 MIN.
TOTAL 17 MIN.

¼ cup canola mayonnaise
1 Tbsp. Dijon mustard
2 tsp. dill pickle relish
8 (1-oz.) slices 10-grain bread, cut in half diagonally
4 small curly leaf lettuce leaves
8 (¼-inch-thick) slices tomato
3 oz. thinly sliced deli no-salt-added roasted turkey
 breast
2 (0.7-oz.) slices reduced-fat Cheddar cheese, cut in
 half diagonally
3 oz. thinly sliced deli 25%-lower-sodium Black
 Forest ham
2 (¾-oz.) slices reduced-fat Swiss cheese, cut in half
 diagonally
8 thinly sliced green bell pepper rings
16 thin slices cucumber
4 pimiento-stuffed Spanish olives (optional)

1. Combine first 3 ingredients. Spread about 1 Tbsp. mayonnaise mixture on 1 side of each of 4 bread triangles. Top with 1 lettuce leaf, 2 tomato slices, ¾ oz. turkey, 1 Cheddar cheese triangle, ¾ oz. ham, 1 Swiss cheese triangle, 2 bell pepper rings, and 4 cucumber slices. Cover sandwiches with remaining bread triangles.

2. Thread 1 olive, if desired, onto each of 4 long wooden picks; secure sandwiches with picks.

## Kitchen Note:

*A Dagwood sandwich, made popular by the comic strip character Dagwood Bumstead, is characterized by layers of sodium- and fat-laden meats and cheeses. We've slimmed ours down by using no-salt-added and lower-sodium deli meats and lower-fat cheeses.*

# Muffuletta

MAKES 6 SERVINGS
HANDS-ON 20 MIN.
TOTAL 20 MIN.

¾ cup chopped assorted olives
¾ cup coarsely chopped jarred artichoke hearts
1 medium carrot, grated
2 Tbsp. chopped fresh basil
1 Tbsp. chopped fresh oregano
3 Tbsp. extra virgin olive oil
1 Tbsp. red wine vinegar
1 garlic clove, minced
1 (16-oz.) ciabatta bread loaf
3 Tbsp. coarse-grained Dijon mustard
½ pound thinly sliced deli porchetta
1 (4-oz.) package thinly sliced Italian chorizo
1 (3-oz.) package thinly sliced prosciutto
8 (1-oz.) provolone cheese slices
⅓ cup sliced red onion
2 cups loosely packed arugula

1. Stir together first 8 ingredients. Add salt and pepper to taste. Cut ciabatta loaf in half lengthwise. Scoop out soft bread from both halves, leaving a ½-inch-thick shell. (Reserve soft center of loaf for another use, if desired.)

2. Spoon olive mixture into bottom half of bread loaf, and spread mustard on top half. Layer meats and cheese slices on top of olive mixture. Top with onions and arugula. Cover with bread top, mustard side down. Cut loaf into wedges or slices.

Note: 1 cup jarred Italian olive salad, drained, may be substituted for olive mixture.

## Make It Easy:

*For a make-ahead twist, wrap the sandwich tightly with plastic wrap, and chill under the weight of a heavy cast-iron skillet up to 8 hours.*

# Greek Chicken Salad

MAKES 4 SERVINGS
HANDS-ON 10 MIN.
TOTAL 10 MIN.

2 cups sliced romaine lettuce
1 cup chopped roasted chicken breast
⅔ cup diced seeded cucumber
¼ cup thinly sliced red onion
¼ cup (1 oz.) crumbled feta cheese
2 Tbsp. fresh lemon juice
2 Tbsp. olive oil
¼ tsp. salt
¼ tsp. freshly ground black pepper
6 Tbsp. roasted red bell pepper hummus
2 (6-inch) whole wheat pitas, cut in half

1. Combine lettuce and next 4 ingredients in a large bowl. Add lemon juice, olive oil, salt, and pepper; toss gently.

2. Spread 1½ Tbsp. hummus inside each pita half; spoon salad mixture evenly into halves. Serve immediately.

## Simple Swap:

*Find prepared hummus in a variety of flavors. Try either spicy three-pepper or artichoke-and-garlic hummus for this sandwich.*

# Confetti Pasta Salad

MAKES 4 TO 6 SERVINGS
HANDS-ON 20 MIN.
TOTAL 25 MIN., INCLUDING VINAIGRETTE

8 oz. cooked pasta
1 pint grape tomatoes, halved
2 cups coarsely chopped fresh spinach
1 yellow bell pepper, chopped
¼ cup finely chopped red onion
3 Tbsp. chopped fresh dill
Fresh Lemon Vinaigrette
1 (4-oz.) package crumbled feta cheese

*1.* Cook pasta according to package directions; drain. Toss pasta with tomatoes and remaining ingredients. Serve immediately, or cover and chill up to 8 hours.

Note: We used small shell pasta in this recipe, but any kind can be used.

**FRESH LEMON VINAIGRETTE**
MAKES ABOUT ¾ CUP
HANDS ON 5 MIN.
TOTAL 5 MIN.

¼ cup fresh lemon juice
1 tsp. Dijon mustard
1 large garlic clove, pressed
¼ tsp. salt
¼ tsp. freshly ground black pepper
½ cup vegetable oil

Whisk together first 5 ingredients. Gradually add oil in a slow, steady stream, whisking until blended.

## Make It Easy:

*You can prepare the Fresh Lemon Vinaigrette ahead, and store in an airtight container in the refrigerator up to 1 week. Bring to room temperature, and whisk before serving.*

# Summer Rolls

## with Peaches and Avocados

MAKES 2 TO 3 SERVINGS (12 TO 16 ROLLS)
HANDS-ON 35 MIN.
TOTAL 45 MIN., INCLUDING SAUCE

12 to 16 (8- to 9-inch) round rice paper sheets
2 small peaches, peeled and thinly sliced
12 to 16 Bibb lettuce leaves
1 English cucumber, cut into thin strips
1 large ripe avocado, thinly sliced
1 lb. shredded barbecued pork (without sauce),
    warm
1 Granny Smith apple, peeled and cut into thin
    strips
1½ cups torn fresh mint, cilantro, and basil
Sweet Pepper-Peanut Sauce

1. Pour hot water to depth of 1 inch into a large
shallow dish. Dip 1 rice paper sheet in hot water
briefly to soften (about 15 to 20 seconds). Pat dry
with paper towels.

2. Place softened rice paper on a flat surface. Place
1 or 2 peach slices in center of rice paper; top with
1 lettuce leaf, 2 cucumber strips, 1 avocado slice,
about 3 Tbsp. pork, 3 or 4 apple strips, and 1½ to
2 Tbsp. herbs. Fold sides over filling, and roll up,
burrito style. Place roll, seam side down, on a
serving platter. Cover with damp paper towels to
keep from drying out.

3. Repeat procedure with remaining rice paper
and filling ingredients. Serve with Sweet Pepper-
Peanut Sauce.

Note: Look for rice paper rounds in the interna-
tional aisle of large grocery stores or at Asian
markets.

SWEET PEPPER-PEANUT SAUCE
MAKES ABOUT 1½ CUPS
HANDS-ON 10 MIN.
TOTAL 10 MIN.

1 cup sweet pepper relish
½ cup cocktail peanuts, finely chopped
3 Tbsp. fresh lime juice
2 Tbsp. lite soy sauce
4 tsp. toasted sesame oil
1 Tbsp. grated fresh ginger
2 green onions, finely chopped
2 garlic cloves, minced
2 tsp. Asian hot chili sauce (such as Sriracha)

Combine all ingredients. Cover and chill until
ready to serve.

## Simple Swap:

**You can use barbecued chicken
or rotisserie chicken in place of
the barbecued pork.**

# Green Tomato Sliders

MAKES 12 SERVINGS
HANDS-ON 20 MIN.
TOTAL 30 MIN.

1½ cups shredded red cabbage
1½ cups shredded napa cabbage
1 cup matchstick carrots
⅓ cup thinly sliced red onion
3 Tbsp. olive oil
2 Tbsp. fresh lime juice
½ cup chopped fresh cilantro, divided
½ cup mayonnaise
2 to 3 tsp. Asian hot chili sauce (such as Sriracha)
12 slider buns or dinner rolls, warmed and split
12 cooked bacon slices
12 fried green tomatoes

1. Stir together first 6 ingredients and ¼ cup cilantro in a medium bowl. Season with salt and pepper to taste. Let stand 10 minutes.

2. Stir together mayonnaise, Asian hot chili sauce, and remaining ¼ cup cilantro. Spread buns with mayonnaise mixture. Top bottom halves of buns with bacon, tomatoes, and cabbage mixture. Cover with top halves of buns, mayonnaise mixture sides down.

## Make It Easy:

*Start with fried green tomatoes from your favorite meat 'n' three restaurant. Secure sweet-hot pickle chips to the bun with wooden picks for a fun garnish.*

## Simple Swap:

*Find gochujang in the Asian section of supermarkets or online at anniechun.com. Or you can substitute 2 tsp. Asian hot chili sauce (such as Sriracha).*

# Cabbage Wraps
## with Sweet-and-Sour Cucumber Salad

MAKES 18 WRAPS
HANDS-ON 25 MIN.
TOTAL 50 MIN., INCLUDING SALAD

Sweet-and-Sour Cucumber Salad
½ cup reduced-sodium soy sauce
¼ cup rice wine vinegar
2 Tbsp. light brown sugar
2 Tbsp. dark sesame oil
2 Tbsp. gochujang (Korean chili paste)
1 Tbsp. grated fresh ginger
1 garlic clove, pressed
1 lb. pulled barbecued pork (without sauce)
18 savoy or napa cabbage leaves
Chopped oil-roasted cocktail peanuts

1. Prepare Sweet-and-Sour Cucumber Salad. While salad chills, process soy sauce and next 6 ingredients in a blender or food processor until smooth.

2. Spoon about ¼ cup pork into each cabbage leaf; drizzle with soy sauce mixture. Spoon Sweet-and-Sour Cucumber Salad over pork, using a slotted spoon. Top with desired amount of peanuts.

### SWEET-AND-SOUR CUCUMBER SALAD
MAKES 8 TO 10 SERVINGS
HANDS-ON 10 MIN.
TOTAL 25 MIN.

3 Tbsp. rice wine vinegar
2 Tbsp. sugar
1 tsp. Dijon mustard
¼ tsp. table salt
¼ tsp. freshly ground black pepper
3 Tbsp. canola oil
1 English cucumber, seeded and thinly sliced into half-moons
2 shallots, minced
2 Tbsp. chopped fresh cilantro

Whisk together vinegar, sugar, Dijon mustard, salt, and pepper in a bowl. Add canola oil in a slow, steady stream, whisking constantly until well blended. Add cucumber, shallots, and cilantro. Toss to coat. Cover and chill 15 minutes.

## Barbecue

**WHAT IT IS:** Barbeque, BBQ, Bar-B-Q, 'Cue, "Q," 'Que (*Bar-bah-q*): noun: A revered cultural experience in the South involving smoky slow-cooked meat, sauce, sweet tea, friends, family, and lots of laughter.

**FIRST THERE'S THE MEAT:** It's got to be cooked carefully for a long time, usually over an open wood fire.

**THEN THERE'S THE SAUCE:** Which kind to use is the real point of controversy. But without the sauce, it just isn't barbecue. Even if the sauce is sloshed on during cooking or stirred into pulled or chopped meat, you have to serve it on the side at the table so folks can add on more.

# Watermelon Salad

## with Smoky Dijon Dressing

MAKES 8 SERVINGS
HANDS-ON 30 MIN.
TOTAL 35 MIN., INCLUDING DRESSING

1 medium-size red onion, sliced
1 cup seasoned rice wine vinegar
1 garlic clove, minced
1 Tbsp. sugar
1½ tsp. salt
12 cups assorted tender salad greens (such as
    mâche, watercress, arugula, and Bibb)
1 cup crumbled Cotija or feta cheese
Smoky Dijon Dressing
8 (1¼-inch-thick) chilled seedless watermelon slices,
    rinds removed
¾ cup salted pepitas or sunflower seeds

1. Stir together first 5 ingredients and ¼ cup water in a glass bowl. Cover and chill 2 hours. (Mixture can be made and chilled up to 2 days ahead.) Remove onions from marinade, discarding marinade.

2. Toss together greens, cheese, 1 cup red onions, and desired amount of dressing in a large bowl. Top each watermelon slice with 1½ cups greens mixture. Sprinkle with pepitas. Serve immediately with remaining vinaigrette and onions.

### SMOKY DIJON DRESSING

MAKES 1 CUP
HANDS ON 5 MIN.
TOTAL 5 MIN.

⅔ cup olive oil
⅓ cup red wine vinegar
2 Tbsp. honey
2 tsp. pimento (Spanish paprika)
2 tsp. coarse-grained Dijon mustard

Combine olive oil and next 4 ingredients. Add salt and pepper to taste.

## Make It Easy:

*If you are short on time, you can substitute your favorite vinaigrette in place of the Smoky Dijon Dressing.*

# Strawberry Caprese

## Bruschetta

MAKES 4 TO 6 SERVINGS
HANDS-ON 20 MIN.
TOTAL 2 HOURS, 50 MIN.

3 Tbsp. white balsamic vinegar
1 small garlic clove, minced
1 Tbsp. light brown sugar
¼ tsp. salt
¼ tsp. freshly ground black pepper
3 Tbsp. olive oil
⅓ cup chopped fresh basil
1 (8-oz.) tub fresh small mozzarella cheese balls
4 cups halved fresh strawberries
Arugula or toasted French bread baguette slices
Garnish: thinly sliced fresh basil

1. Whisk together white balsamic vinegar, minced garlic, brown sugar, salt, and pepper in a large bowl until sugar is dissolved. Add olive oil in a slow, steady stream, whisking constantly until smooth. Add ⅓ cup chopped fresh basil and mozzarella cheese balls; toss to coat. Cover and chill 2 hours.

2. Stir in strawberries; let stand at room temperature 30 minutes, stirring occasionally. Serve over fresh arugula or as an appetizer with toasted French bread baguette slices. Garnish with thinly sliced fresh basil.

### Make It Easy:

*The vinaigrette can be mixed and chilled ahead. Make a double batch to use on salads throughout the week.*

# Panzanella Salad

MAKES 4 SERVINGS
HANDS-ON 10 MIN.
TOTAL 10 MIN.

1 Tbsp. vegetable oil
3 Tbsp. white balsamic vinegar
⅛ tsp. salt
¼ tsp. black pepper
6½ cups chopped tomato (3 very large)
1½ cups cubed English cucumber
½ cup pitted kalamata olives
½ cup fresh basil leaves, torn
6 oz. whole wheat country-style bread, torn into
      bite-size pieces (4 cups)
1 (4-oz.) package crumbled feta cheese

*1.* Combine first 4 ingredients in a large bowl, stirring with a whisk. Stir in tomato and next 3 ingredients. Add bread and cheese; toss gently. Serve immediately.

## Simple Swap:

*Like many Italian dishes, panzanella (pahn-zah-NEHL-lah) was probably first made out of necessity—combining stale bread with readily available fresh garden vegetables. You can use cornbread or a white bread in place of the whole wheat bread. If you prefer a drier panzanella, toast the bread before tossing it with the tomato mixture.*

# Pimiento Cheese

MAKES **ABOUT 6 CUPS**
HANDS-ON 15 MIN.
TOTAL 15 MIN.

1 (12-oz.) jar roasted red bell peppers, drained and
   finely chopped
1 cup mayonnaise
¼ cup red onion, finely chopped
¼ cup fresh parsley, chopped
1 Tbsp. fresh dill, chopped
2 Tbsp. Dijon mustard
2 Tbsp. jarred pepperoncini salad peppers
1 Tbsp. liquid from pepperoncini salad peppers
1 tsp. grated fresh horseradish
4 cups shredded sharp Cheddar cheese
3 cups shredded Havarti cheese

*1.* Stir together finely chopped roasted red bell peppers and the next 8 ingredients. Gently stir in sharp Cheddar cheese and Havarti cheese until well blended. Cover and chill until ready to serve.

### Make It Easy:

*If you're pressed for time, purchase your favorite pimiento cheese from the grocery store and stir in the finely chopped roasted red peppers and pepperoncini salad peppers and juice for extra flavor.*

# Salmon Salad
## with Avocado

**MAKES 6 TO 8 SERVINGS**
**HANDS-ON 15 MIN.**
**TOTAL 15 MIN.**

¼ cup olive oil
3 Tbsp. fresh lemon juice
1 tsp. Dijon mustard
¾ tsp. sugar
½ tsp. kosher salt
¼ tsp. freshly ground black pepper
1 (5-oz.) package arugula, thoroughly washed*
6 radishes, thinly sliced
2 (4-oz.) packages thinly sliced smoked salmon
1 avocado, sliced

1. Whisk together first 6 ingredients. Gently toss together arugula, radishes, and half of olive oil mixture in a large bowl. Arrange on a serving platter with salmon and avocado. Serve immediately with remaining olive oil mixture.

*1 (5-oz.) package spring mix, thoroughly washed, may be substituted.

## Make It Easy:

**Packaged smoked salmon and prepackaged arugula make this dinner come together in just 15 minutes.**

# Crab Salad

## with Peaches and Avocados

MAKES 6 SERVINGS
HANDS-ON 30 MIN.
TOTAL 30 MIN.

1 lb. fresh jumbo lump crabmeat
2 Tbsp. lemon zest
1 Tbsp. mayonnaise
½ tsp. dry mustard
5 Tbsp. fresh lemon juice, divided
½ jalapeño pepper, seeded and finely diced
¼ cup finely diced celery
2 green onions, finely chopped
White pepper
5 to 6 medium peaches (about 1¾ lb.),
    unpeeled and coarsely chopped
1 Tbsp. honey
3 medium avocados, diced
Arugula

1. Pick crabmeat, removing any bits of shell. Whisk together lemon zest, next 2 ingredients, and 1 Tbsp. lemon juice. Fold in jalapeño pepper, next 2 ingredients, and crabmeat, using a rubber spatula. Season with kosher salt and white pepper to taste.

2. Stir together peaches and remaining 4 Tbsp. lemon juice. Reserve 3 cups peach mixture. Pulse honey and remaining peach mixture in a food processor 8 to 10 times or until smooth. Season pureed peach mixture with kosher salt and white pepper to taste.

3. Spoon ¼ cup pureed peach mixture onto a chilled plate. Place a 3½-inch round cutter in center of peach mixture on plate. (A clean, empty tuna can with both ends removed may be used instead.) Spoon one-sixth of diced avocados and ½ cup reserved chopped peach mixture into cutter, packing each layer firmly and sprinkling with kosher salt and white pepper to taste. Top with about ½ cup crab mixture. Carefully remove cutter from plate. Repeat procedure with remaining pureed peach mixture, avocado, chopped peach mixture, and crab mixture. Arrange desired amount of arugula around each layered salad; serve immediately.

## Make It Easy:

*Make the crab salad ahead, but the avocado and peach layers are best prepared just before serving.*

# Picnic in a Glass

MAKES 6 TO 8 SERVINGS
HANDS-ON 20 MIN.
TOTAL 3 HOURS

1 (19-oz.) can chickpeas, drained and rinsed
2 Tbsp. chopped fresh flat-leaf parsley
2 Tbsp. chopped fresh mint
2 Tbsp. fresh lemon juice
5 Tbsp. olive oil, divided
1 (2½- to 3-lb.) whole deli-roasted chicken, skinned,
    boned, and shredded
¾ cup chopped radishes
¼ cup finely chopped red onion
1 pt. grape tomatoes, halved
1½ cups chopped English cucumbers
Yogurt Dressing
3 cups coarsely crushed pita chips
Lemon wedges

1. Stir together first 4 ingredients and 2 Tbsp. olive
   oil; stir in shredded chicken. Add salt and black
   pepper to taste; let stand 15 minutes.

2. Meanwhile, stir together radishes, onion, and 1
   Tbsp. olive oil. Stir together tomatoes and 1 Tbsp.
   olive oil. Stir together cucumbers and remaining 1
   Tbsp. olive oil. Season each mixture with salt and
   pepper to taste.

3. Layer chickpea mixture, radish mixture, ¾ cup
   Yogurt Dressing, tomato mixture, pita chips, and
   cucumber mixture in a 4-qt. bowl; top with
   remaining Yogurt Dressing. Cover and chill 2 to
   4 hours. Serve with lemon wedges and additional
   pita chips.

## YOGURT DRESSING

MAKES ABOUT 2½ CUPS
HANDS-ON 10 MIN.
TOTAL 25 MIN.

Stir together 1 cup Greek yogurt; 4 oz. feta cheese,
finely crumbled; 2 Tbsp. chopped fresh dill; 5 Tbsp.
buttermilk; 2 tsp. lemon zest; 2 Tbsp. fresh lemon
juice; and 1 garlic clove, minced. Add table salt and
black pepper to taste. Let stand 15 minutes.

## Make It Easy:

*This Southern spin on Middle Eastern fattoush salad can be assembled in advance so the flavors meld and pita chips soften. Serve it directly from the jars. We love wide-mouth Weck jars, although any style will do.*

# Black-Eyed Pea Salad

MAKES 6 SERVINGS

HANDS-ON 20 MIN.

TOTAL 10 HOURS, 5 MIN.

¼ cup chopped fresh cilantro
¼ cup red pepper jelly
¼ cup red wine vinegar
2 Tbsp. olive oil
1 jalapeño pepper, seeded and minced
¾ tsp. salt
¼ tsp. black pepper
1 (15 ½-oz.) can black-eyed peas, drained and rinsed
1 cup diced red bell pepper
⅓ cup diced red onion
2 large fresh peaches, peeled and diced
2 cups torn watercress

1. Whisk together cilantro and next 6 ingredients in a large bowl. Add drained black-eyed peas, bell pepper, and onion, tossing to coat; cover and chill 8 hours. Stir peaches and watercress into pea mixture just before serving.

## Kitchen Note:

*Ripen peaches quickly by placing them in a brown paper bag at room temperature until fragrant and juicy.*

# Texas Caviar

MAKES 4 TO 6 SERVINGS
HANDS-ON 20 MIN.
TOTAL 45 MIN., INCLUDING VINAIGRETTE

1 (15.8-oz.) can black-eyed peas, drained and rinsed
1 (15-oz.) can black beans, drained and rinsed
⅓ cup finely chopped roasted red bell peppers
¼ cup finely chopped poblano pepper
Texas Vinaigrette, divided
2 (8.8-oz.) pouches fully cooked basmati rice
1¼ cups halved grape tomatoes
1 cup (4 oz.) shredded pepper Jack cheese
¾ cup loosely packed fresh cilantro leaves
⅔ cup thinly sliced celery
⅓ cup thinly sliced green onions
Tortilla chips
Garnish: sliced pickled jalapeño peppers

*1.* Stir together first 4 ingredients and ¼ cup Texas Vinaigrette in a microwave-safe glass bowl; let stand 20 minutes, stirring occasionally. Microwave at HIGH 2 minutes or until thoroughly heated, stirring at 30-second intervals.

*2.* Heat rice according to package directions; fluff with a fork. Divide bean mixture, rice, tomatoes, and next 4 ingredients among 4 to 6 individual plates. Serve with tortilla chips and remaining vinaigrette.

Note: We tested with Tasty Bite Basmati Rice.

**TEXAS VINAIGRETTE**
MAKES ABOUT 1 CUP
HANDS-ON 5 MIN.
TOTAL 5 MIN.

½ cup olive oil
¼ cup fresh lime juice
2 Tbsp. chopped fresh cilantro
1 Tbsp. hot sauce
1 garlic clove, minced
½ tsp. chili powder
½ tsp. ground cumin

Whisk together olive oil, lime juice, cilantro, hot sauce, garlic, chili powder, and cumin. Add salt and pepper to taste.

## Kitchen Note:

*Customize with any topping, such as guacamole, salsa, or a dollop of sour cream.*

# Salmon Tostadas
## with Zucchini-Radish Slaw

MAKES 4 TO 6 SERVINGS
HANDS-ON 20 MIN.
TOTAL 35 MIN.

½ cup sour cream
1 tsp. lime zest
1 garlic clove, minced
¼ tsp. ground chipotle chile pepper
1 Tbsp. fresh lime juice
2½ cups shredded savoy cabbage
1 cup grated zucchini
5 radishes, thinly sliced
⅓ cup loosely packed fresh cilantro leaves
1 jalapeño pepper, thinly sliced
2 Tbsp. olive oil
3 Tbsp. fresh lime juice
1 to 2 (4-oz.) hot-smoked salmon fillets
6 tostada shells
1 avocado

*1.* Stir together sour cream, lime zest, garlic, ground chipotle chile pepper, lime juice, and salt and pepper to taste.

*2.* Toss together cabbage, zucchini, radishes, cilantro, jalapeño pepper, olive oil, lime juice, and salt and pepper to taste. Let stand 15 minutes.

*3.* Flake salmon into pieces, discarding skin. Spread sour cream mixture over tostada shells, and top with salmon and cabbage mixture. Cut avocado into 6 wedges. Top tostadas with avocado wedges; serve immediately.

## Simple Swap:

**Use smoked trout in place of the salmon fillets.**

# Quick Pickled Shrimp

MAKES 6 TO 8 SERVINGS
HANDS-ON 10 MIN.
TOTAL 2 HOURS, 10 MIN.

1 lemon, thinly sliced
⅓ cup thinly sliced red onion
¼ cup olive oil
3 Tbsp. red wine vinegar
2 Tbsp. chopped fresh dill
2 Tbsp. chopped fresh flat-leaf parsley
1¼ tsp. Creole seasoning
1 garlic clove, minced
1 lb. peeled, medium-size cooked shrimp

*1.* Stir together lemon slices, onion, olive oil, vinegar, dill, parsley, Creole seasoning, and garlic in a large bowl; transfer to a zip-top plastic freezer bag. Add shrimp, turning to coat. Seal and chill 2 to 6 hours.

*2.* Remove shrimp, discarding marinade. Sprinkle shrimp with salt and pepper to taste.

## Kitchen Note:

**Perk up precooked shrimp by simply tossing them in very hot water for 30 seconds. Then plunge immediately into ice water to stop the cooking process. Drain well.**

# Shrimp Salad

## with Artichokes

MAKES 8 SERVINGS
HANDS-ON 15 MIN.
TOTAL 8 HOURS, 15 MIN.

¼ cup white balsamic vinegar
2 Tbsp. finely chopped fresh parsley
2 Tbsp. finely chopped green onion
3 Tbsp. olive oil
1 (0.75-oz.) envelope garlic-and-herb dressing mix
1 lb. peeled and deveined, large cooked shrimp (21/30 count)
1 (14-oz.) can artichoke hearts, drained and cut in half
1 (6-oz.) can large black olives, drained and rinsed
1 cup halved grape tomatoes
1 (4-oz.) package feta cheese, cut into ½-inch cubes
Small fresh basil leaves

1. Whisk together balsamic vinegar and next 4 ingredients in a bowl. Stir in shrimp and next 4 ingredients. Cover and chill 8 to 24 hours.

2. Stir in desired amount of basil just before serving. Serve with a slotted spoon.

Note: We tested with Good Seasons Garlic & Herb Salad Dressing & Recipe Mix.

## Make It Easy:

**To quickly chop green onions, use a chef's knife to cut off the outer parts of the onion. Then continue to chop the pieces, using a rocking motion.**

# Zucchini "Linguine"
## with Mushrooms

MAKES 4 MAIN-DISH OR 6 TO 8
SIDE-DISH SERVINGS
HANDS-ON 20 MIN.
TOTAL 50 MIN.

1 (3.5-oz.) package fresh shiitake mushrooms*
⅓ cup extra virgin olive oil
2 Tbsp. fresh lemon juice
½ shallot, minced
½ tsp. table salt
½ tsp. freshly ground black pepper
1½ lb. small zucchini
3 Tbsp. thinly sliced chives
3 Tbsp. chopped fresh basil
⅓ cup chopped toasted, salted pecans
Freshly grated pecorino or Parmesan cheese

*1.* Cut stems from mushrooms and, if desired, reserve for another use. Cut mushroom caps into thin slices. Whisk together olive oil and next 4 ingredients in a large bowl. Stir in mushrooms; let stand 10 minutes.

*2.* Meanwhile, cut zucchini lengthwise into ⅛- to ¼-inch-thick slices. Stack 2 or 3 slices on a cutting board, and cut lengthwise into thin strips (similar to linguine). Repeat with remaining zucchini.

*3.* Toss zucchini in olive oil mixture. Let stand 20 minutes, stirring occasionally. Fold in chives and basil. Transfer to a serving platter; sprinkle with pecans and cheese. Serve immediately.

* ½ (8-oz.) package button mushrooms may be substituted.

## Simple Swap:

**Cutting zucchini into thin strips is easy and makes a fresh substitute for pasta. Add thinly sliced ribbons of salami for a meatier meal.**

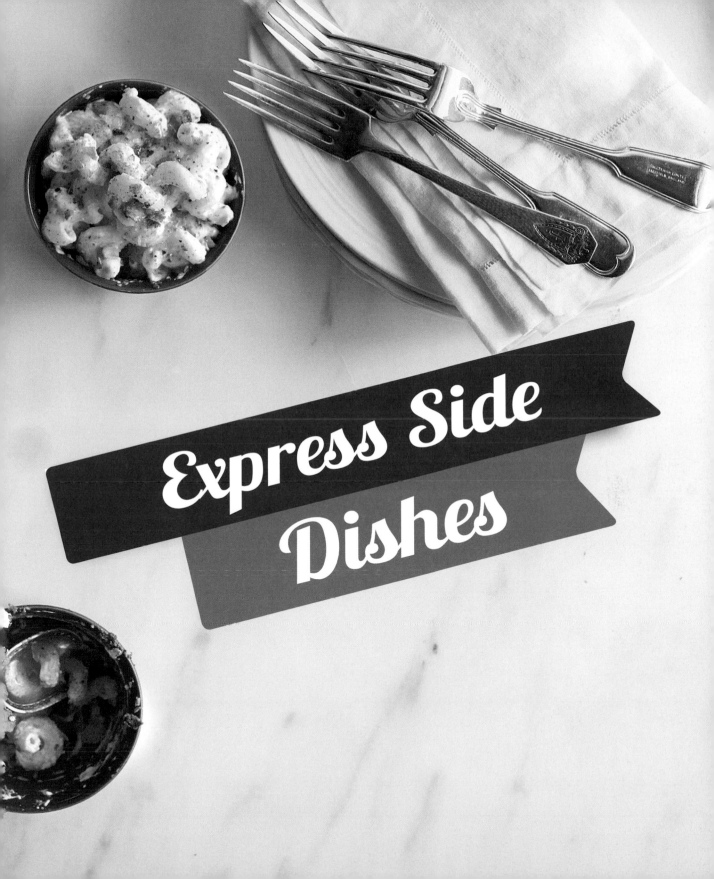

# Express Side Dishes

# Peach-Ginger Slaw

MAKES 8 SERVINGS
HANDS-ON 20 MIN.
TOTAL 30 MIN.

1 cup chopped pecans
3 Tbsp. pepper jelly
¼ cup rice wine vinegar
1 Tbsp. sesame oil
1 tsp. grated fresh ginger
⅓ cup canola oil
1 (16-oz.) package shredded coleslaw mix
2 large fresh peaches, unpeeled and coarsely
     chopped (about 2 cups)

*1.* Preheat oven to 350°. Bake pecans in a single layer in a shallow pan 10 to 12 minutes or until toasted and fragrant, stirring halfway through. Cool completely (about 10 minutes).

*2.* Meanwhile, microwave jelly in a large microwave-safe bowl at HIGH 15 seconds. Whisk in vinegar and next 2 ingredients until blended. Gradually add canola oil in a slow, steady stream, whisking constantly until well blended.

*3.* Add coleslaw mix, and toss to coat. Gently stir in peaches. Stir in pecans; add salt to taste. Serve immediately, or cover and chill up to 8 hours, stirring in pecans and salt to taste just before serving.

## Simple Swap:

**Substitute almonds for the pecans. Toast them for 5 to 6 minutes.**

# Applesauce

MAKES ABOUT 6 CUPS
HANDS-ON 20 MIN.
TOTAL 20 MIN.

12 large apples, peeled and coarsely chopped
1 cup sugar
½ lemon, sliced

1. Cook all ingredients in a Dutch oven over medium heat, stirring often, 20 minutes or until apples are tender and juices thicken. Remove and discard lemon slices.

2. Serve applesauce warm; or let cool, and store in an airtight container in the refrigerator for up to 2 weeks.

**VARIATION: SPICED APPLESAUCE**
Substitute ½ cup firmly packed brown sugar and ½ cup granulated sugar for 1 cup sugar. Omit lemon slices, and add 1 tsp. ground cinnamon and ¼ tsp. ground cloves; prepare as directed.

## Kitchen Note:

*For the best taste and texture, use a variety of apples—such as Granny Smith, Golden Delicious, and Gala—when making applesauce.*

# Fennel Salad
## with Watermelon

MAKES ABOUT 6 CUPS
HANDS-ON 10 MIN.
TOTAL 10 MIN.

3 Tbsp. fresh lime juice
2 Tbsp. olive oil
1 Tbsp. honey
¼ tsp. kosher salt
¼ tsp. freshly ground black pepper
3 ¼ cups thinly sliced fennel bulb
3 cups cubed watermelon
¼ cup chopped fresh mint
2 oz. (about ½ cup) crumbled feta cheese

1. Combine first 5 ingredients, stirring with a whisk. Combine fennel and watermelon in a large bowl. Drizzle dressing over watermelon mixture; toss gently. Sprinkle with mint and cheese.

## Kitchen Note:

**You can also pair the Honey-Lime Vinaigrette with grilled shrimp or chicken.**

# Tortellini Pasta Salad

MAKES ABOUT 3 SERVINGS
HANDS-ON 15 MIN.
TOTAL 15 MIN.

1 (9-oz.) package fresh cheese tortellini
2 cups (1-inch) sliced asparagus (about ½ pound)
2 tsp. olive oil
2 garlic cloves, minced
1 (6-oz.) package fresh baby spinach
¼ tsp. salt
¼ tsp. black pepper
2 tsp. fresh lemon juice
3 Tbsp. shaved fresh Parmesan cheese
3 Tbsp. pine nuts, toasted

*1.* Prepare tortellini according to package directions, omitting salt and fat. Add asparagus during last 3 minutes of cooking. Drain pasta and asparagus; rinse with cold water.

*2.* While pasta cooks, heat oil in a large nonstick skillet over medium heat. Add garlic; sauté 1 minute. Add spinach, salt, and pepper; cook 2 minutes or until spinach wilts.

*3.* Combine pasta mixture and spinach mixture in a large bowl. Add lemon juice; toss gently to coat. Top servings with cheese and nuts.

## Make It Easy:

**Cook the asparagus with the pasta to save prep time and cleanup time by using only one pot.**

# Cucumber Salad

## with Tomatoes

MAKES 8 SERVINGS
HANDS-ON 10 MIN.
TOTAL 20 MIN.

⅓ cup olive oil
¼ cup red wine vinegar
1 Tbsp. fresh lemon juice
¾ tsp. salt
½ tsp. black pepper
4 cups grape tomatoes, halved
2½ cups sliced seedless or English cucumber
¼ cup chopped fresh parsley
¼ cup thinly sliced sweet onion
2 Tbsp. chopped fresh oregano

*1.* Whisk together first 5 ingredients in a large bowl. Add tomatoes and remaining ingredients; toss well.

*2.* Let stand at least 10 minutes before serving to allow the flavors to infuse.

### Simple Swap:

*Substitute red onions for sweet onions. They have a milder, less pungent flavor and an attractive purple hue.*

# Fresh Corn Quinoa

**MAKES 4 SERVINGS**
**HANDS-ON 15 MIN.**
**TOTAL 30 MIN.**

1½ cups uncooked red quinoa
½ tsp. kosher salt
4 shallots or 2 small onions, quartered
1 Tbsp. olive oil
2 garlic cloves, minced
2 cups fresh corn kernels
6 cups shredded greens (such as chard)
½ cup torn basil
¼ cup torn mint
2 Tbsp. fresh lemon juice
Garnish: fresh rosemary

*1.* Bring quinoa, salt, and 4 cups water to a boil. Cover, reduce heat to medium, and simmer 8 to 10 minutes or until tender; drain. Cover and let stand 15 minutes.

*2.* Meanwhile, sauté shallots in hot olive oil in a large skillet over medium heat 3 minutes or until tender. Add garlic; sauté 1 minute. Add corn kernels and shredded greens; cook 2 minutes or just until wilted. Add quinoa, basil, mint, and fresh lemon juice.

## Kitchen Note:

*Quinoa tends to hold lots of water, so be sure to use a fine-mesh strainer to thoroughly and quickly drain it.*

# Mac 'n' Cheese
## with Andouille Sausage

MAKES 10 TO 12 SERVINGS
HANDS-ON 35 MIN.
TOTAL 1 HOUR

1 (16-oz.) package cavatappi pasta
1 Tbsp. salt
½ pound andouille sausage, casings removed
4 cups heavy cream
1 (16-oz.) package processed cheese, cut into 1-inch
    cubes
2 cups (8 oz.) freshly shredded smoked Cheddar
    cheese
½ cup freshly shredded aged Gouda cheese
½ cup freshly shredded Parmigiano-Reggiano
    cheese
1 (5-oz.) package unsalted kettle-cooked potato
    chips, crumbled

*1.* Preheat oven to 375°. Prepare pasta according
    to package directions for al dente, adding salt to
    water.

*2.* Meanwhile, cut sausage lengthwise into quarters.
    Cut each quarter into ¼-inch-thick pieces.

*3.* Sauté sausage in a Dutch oven over medium-high
    heat 3 minutes or until browned around edges;
    drain on paper towels.

*4.* Bring cream to a simmer in Dutch oven over
    medium-high heat; reduce heat to low, and stir in
    processed cheese. Cook, stirring constantly, until
    cheese is melted. Stir in sausage and remaining
    cheeses; cook, stirring constantly, until cheeses
    are melted. Remove from heat; stir in hot cooked
    pasta.

*5.* Pour mixture into a buttered 3-qt. baking dish or
    12 (8-oz.) ramekins; top with potato chips. Bake at
    375° for 20 minutes or until bubbly and browned.
    Remove from oven, and let stand 5 minutes.

## Simple Swap:

*Use lightly salted potato chips
in place of the kettle-cooked
potato chips.*

# Pan-Fried Okra

## with Onion and Tomatoes

MAKES 8 SERVINGS
HANDS-ON 20 MIN.
TOTAL 20 MIN.

2 lbs. fresh okra
½ cup vegetable oil
1 medium-size red onion, thinly sliced
2 large tomatoes, seeded and thinly sliced
2 Tbsp. lime juice
1½ tsp. salt
1½ tsp. black pepper
1 tsp. chicken bouillon granules

1. Cut okra in half lengthwise.

2. Pour ¼ cup oil into a large skillet over medium-high heat. Cook okra in hot oil, in batches, 6 minutes or until browned, turning occasionally. Remove from skillet, and drain well on paper towels. Repeat with remaining okra, adding remaining ¼ cup oil as needed. Cool.

3. Stir together onion and next 5 ingredients in a large bowl; add okra, tossing to coat. Serve at room temperature.

## Kitchen Note:

**Remove the tip of the okra stem before cutting the pod in half.**

**Kitchen Note:**

Select green beans that are crisp and firm with no signs of discoloration. Store them in a plastic bag in the refrigerator.

# Green Beans
## with Goat Cheese and Tomatoes

**MAKES 6 TO 8 SERVINGS**
**HANDS-ON 20 MIN.**
**TOTAL 20 MIN.**

½ cup sliced almonds
2 lbs. haricots verts (thin green beans), trimmed
3 Tbsp. sherry vinegar*
2 Tbsp. fresh lemon juice
¾ tsp. salt
½ tsp. black pepper
⅓ cup olive oil
1 pt. cherry tomatoes, halved
2 shallots, thinly sliced
2 garlic cloves, minced
½ (4-oz.) goat cheese log, crumbled

1. Preheat oven to 350°. Bake almonds in a single layer in a shallow pan 6 to 8 minutes or until lightly toasted and fragrant, stirring halfway through.

2. Cook green beans in boiling salted water to cover 6 to 8 minutes or until crisp-tender; drain. Plunge beans into ice water to stop the cooking process; drain.

3. Whisk together vinegar and next 3 ingredients in a large bowl; add olive oil in a slow, steady stream, whisking constantly until blended and smooth. Add cherry tomatoes, shallots, garlic, and green beans; toss to coat.

4. Top green bean mixture with crumbled goat cheese and toasted almonds.

*White wine vinegar may be substituted.

## Tomatoes

**SEASON:** May through September in the most temperate regions; June through August is peak season nationwide.

**CHOOSING:** Look for tomatoes with a bright, shiny skin and firm flesh that yields slightly to gentle pressure.

**STORING:** Store them at room temperature but not in direct sunlight—the kitchen windowsill may not be the best spot. Never store tomatoes in the refrigerator. The cold destroys flavor and leaves tomatoes with a mealy texture.

**GROWING:** Tomato plants need full sun and flourish with several gallons of water a week. When growing in containers, ensure the pots are at least 24 inches in diameter. Deep roots are the secret to keeping plants well watered and healthy.

# Maque Choux

MAKES 8 SERVINGS
HANDS-ON 18 MIN.
TOTAL 18 MIN.

¼ lb. spicy smoked sausage, diced
½ cup chopped sweet onion
½ cup chopped green bell pepper
2 garlic cloves, minced
3 cups fresh corn kernels
1 cup sliced fresh okra
1 cup peeled, seeded, and diced tomato (½ lb.)

1. Sauté sausage in a large skillet over medium-high heat 3 minutes or until browned. Add onion, bell pepper, and garlic, and sauté 5 minutes or until tender.

2. Add corn, okra, and tomato; cook, stirring often, 10 minutes. Season with salt and pepper to taste.

Note: We tested with Conecuh Original Spicy and Hot Smoked Sausage.

## Simple Swap:

*If you don't like spicy food, you can substitute the sausage with a milder version to suit your tastes.*

# Green Peas
## with Crispy Bacon

MAKES 6 SERVINGS
HANDS-ON 37 MIN.
TOTAL TIME 37 MIN.

4 bacon slices
2 shallots, diced
1 tsp. orange zest
1 cup fresh orange juice
1 tsp. freshly ground black pepper
½ tsp. salt
2 (16-oz.) bags frozen sweet green peas, thawed*
1 tsp. butter
1 Tbsp. chopped fresh mint
Garnish: orange rind curls

1. Cook bacon in a medium skillet until crisp; remove and drain on paper towels, reserving 1 tsp. drippings in skillet. Crumble bacon, and set aside.

2. Sauté shallots in hot bacon drippings over medium-high heat 2 minutes or until tender. Stir in orange zest, orange juice, pepper, and salt. Cook, stirring occasionally, 5 minutes or until reduced by half. Add peas, and cook 5 more minutes; stir in butter and mint.

3. Transfer peas to a serving dish, and sprinkle with crumbled bacon.

*6 cups shelled fresh sweet green peas may be substituted. Cook peas in boiling water to cover 5 minutes; drain and proceed with recipe as directed.

## Kitchen Note

**Mint and orange brighten the flavor of this simple side dish. When in season, use fresh peas.**

# Feta-Stuffed Tomatoes

MAKES 8 SERVINGS
HANDS-ON 15 MIN.
TOTAL 30 MIN.

4 large tomatoes
4 oz. crumbled feta cheese
¼ cup fine, dry breadcrumbs
2 Tbsp. chopped green onions
2 Tbsp. chopped fresh flat-leaf parsley
2 Tbsp. olive oil
¼ tsp. salt
¼ tsp. black pepper
Garnish: chopped fresh flat-leaf parsley

*1.* Preheat oven to 350°.

*2.* Cut tomatoes in half horizontally. Scoop out pulp from each tomato half, leaving shells intact; discard seeds and coarsely chop pulp.

*3.* Stir together pulp, feta cheese, and next 6 ingredients in a bowl. Taste to make sure the mixture is properly seasoned. Spoon mixture into tomato shells, and place in a 13- x 9-inch baking dish.

*4.* Bake at 350° for 15 minutes.

## Kitchen Note

*Shop for plump, juicy tomatoes at your local farmers' market during the summer—it's the best time of year to enjoy their flavor. In the winter, choose Roma tomatoes.*

# Hot Potato Salad

## with Green Beans and Bacon

MAKES 8 SERVINGS
HANDS-ON 50 MIN.
TOTAL 50 MIN.

3 lbs. fingerling potatoes, cut in half
1 (8-oz.) package haricots verts (thin green beans)
½ cup white wine vinegar
1 shallot, minced
3 Tbsp. honey
1 Tbsp. Dijon mustard
1½ tsp. salt
1 tsp. black pepper
½ cup olive oil
2 Tbsp. chopped fresh dill
¼ cup coarsely chopped fresh parsley
4 fully cooked bacon slices, chopped

1. Bring potatoes and water to cover to a boil in a large Dutch oven over medium-high heat, and cook 20 minutes or until tender. Drain.

2. Meanwhile, cook green beans in boiling water to cover in a medium saucepan 3 to 4 minutes or until crisp-tender. Plunge in ice water to stop the cooking process; drain.

3. Whisk together vinegar and next 5 ingredients in a medium bowl. Add oil in a slow, steady stream, whisking constantly, until smooth.

4. Pour vinegar mixture over potatoes. Just before serving, add green beans, dill, and parsley, and toss gently until blended. Sprinkle with bacon. Serve immediately, or cover and chill until ready to serve.

## Make It Easy:

*Using prepackaged haricots verts and fully cooked bacon makes this favorite side dish come together in a hurry.*

# Corn on the Cob

## with Jalapeño and Lime

**MAKES 8 SERVINGS**
**HANDS-ON 30 MIN.**
**TOTAL 30 MIN.**

8 ears fresh corn, husks removed
Vegetable cooking spray
½ cup butter, softened
1 jalapeño pepper, seeded and minced
1 small garlic clove, pressed
1 Tbsp. lime zest
1 tsp. fresh lime juice
2 tsp. chopped fresh cilantro
Garnish: lime zest

*1.* Preheat grill to 350° to 400° (medium-high) heat. Coat corn lightly with cooking spray. Sprinkle with salt and pepper to taste. Grill corn, covered with grill lid, 15 minutes or until golden brown, turning occasionally.

*2.* Meanwhile, stir together butter and next 5 ingredients. Remove corn from grill. Serve corn with butter mixture.

### Kitchen Note:

**To make it a meal, toss a steak or chicken breast on the grill while the corn cooks.**

# Sweet Potato Stacks

MAKES 12 SERVINGS
HANDS-ON 25 MIN.
TOTAL 1 HOUR, 5 MIN.

1½ pounds small sweet potatoes, peeled and thinly
    sliced
2 tsp. chopped fresh thyme, divided
1 cup (4 oz.) freshly shredded mozzarella cheese,
    divided
⅔ cup heavy cream
1 garlic clove, pressed
½ to ¾ tsp. salt
¼ tsp. freshly ground black pepper
Garnish: fresh thyme

1. Preheat oven to 375°. Layer half of sweet potatoes
   in a lightly greased 12-cup muffin pan. Sprinkle
   with 1½ tsp. thyme and ½ cup cheese. Top with
   remaining sweet potatoes. (Potatoes will come
   slightly above the rim of each cup.)

2. Microwave cream, next 3 ingredients, and
   remaining ½ tsp. thyme at HIGH 1 minute. Pour
   cream mixture into muffin cups (about 1 Tbsp.
   per cup).

3. Bake at 375°, covered with aluminum foil, 30 minutes. Uncover and sprinkle with remaining ½ cup
   cheese. Bake 5 to 7 minutes or until cheese is
   melted and slightly golden.

4. Let stand 5 minutes. Run a sharp knife around
   rim of each cup, and lift potato stacks from cups
   using a spoon or thin spatula. Transfer to a serving
   platter.

## Kitchen Note:

*Each muffin cup flares
slightly, so stack slices from
ends of potatoes in the bottom
and use wider slices from
the middle of the sweet potato
at the top.*

# Oven "Fried" Potatoes

MAKES 4 SERVINGS
HANDS-ON 15 MIN.
TOTAL 55 MIN.

1½ lb. medium-size baking potatoes,
    peeled and cut into ½-inch-thick strips
1 Tbsp. vegetable oil
½ tsp. kosher or table salt

*1.* Preheat oven to 450°. Rinse potatoes in cold water. Drain and thoroughly pat dry. Toss together potatoes, oil, and salt in a large bowl.

*2.* Place a lightly greased wire rack in a sheet tray. Arrange potatoes in a single layer on wire rack, ensuring they are not crowded together.

*3.* Bake at 450° for 40 to 45 minutes or until browned. Serve immediately.

## Simple Swap:

*To make Italian-Parmesan Oven Fries, toss 2 tsp. freshly ground Italian seasoning with potato mixture, and bake as directed. Sprinkle warm fries with 2 Tbsp. grated Parmesan.*

# Roasted Sweet Potatoes

MAKES **ABOUT 7 SERVINGS**
HANDS-ON **10 MIN.**
TOTAL **35 MIN.**

2¾ **pounds sweet potatoes, peeled and cut**
    **into 1-inch pieces**
2 **Tbsp. olive oil**
1 **tsp. light brown sugar**
1 **tsp. chili powder**
½ **tsp. kosher salt**
¼ **tsp. freshly ground black pepper**

*1.* Preheat oven to 450°.

*2.* Place sweet potatoes on a 17- x 12-inch baking pan. Drizzle with oil; toss with a spatula until coated. Combine brown sugar and remaining ingredients in a small bowl. Sprinkle brown sugar mixture over potato, tossing to coat.

*3.* Bake at 450° for 20 minutes; turn with a spatula. Bake 5 more minutes or until tender.

## Make It Easy:

*Peel and cut the potatoes the night before so all you have to do is toss a few ingredients together before putting them in the oven.*

# Fried Cucumbers

MAKES ABOUT 5½ TO 6 DOZEN
HANDS-ON 37 MIN.
TOTAL 57 MIN.

4 small Kirby cucumbers (about 1 lb.),
    cut into ⅛- to ¼-inch-thick slices
1 tsp. kosher salt, divided
¾ cup cornstarch
½ cup self-rising white cornmeal mix
¼ tsp. ground black pepper
¼ tsp. ground red pepper
¾ cup lemon-lime soft drink
1 large egg, lightly beaten
Vegetable oil
Ranch dressing or desired sauce

*1.* Arrange cucumber slices between layers of paper towels. Sprinkle with ½ tsp. kosher salt, and let stand 20 minutes.

*2.* Combine cornstarch and next 3 ingredients. Stir in soft drink and egg. Dip cucumber slices into batter.

*3.* Pour oil to depth of ½ inch into a large cast-iron or heavy skillet; heat to 375°. Fry cucumbers, 6 to 8 at a time, about 1½ minutes on each side or until golden. Drain on paper towels. Sprinkle with remaining ½ tsp. kosher salt, and serve immediately with dressing or sauce.

Note: We tested with White Lily Self-Rising White Cornmeal Mix.

## Make It Easy:

**Use a mandolin slicer to make quick work of slicing the cucumbers.**

# Black-Eyed Pea Cakes

MAKES 6 SERVINGS
HANDS-ON 20 MIN.
TOTAL 20 MIN.

1 (15-oz.) can seasoned black-eyed peas, undrained
2 garlic cloves, microplaned
½ tsp. salt
1 (6-oz.) package buttermilk cornbread mix
1 large egg, lightly beaten
¼ cup sour cream
1½ tsp. Southwest chipotle salt-free seasoning blend

1. Coarsely mash peas with fork. Stir in garlic and next 5 ingredients until blended.

2. Spoon about ⅓ cup batter for each cake onto a hot, lightly greased griddle. Cook cakes 2 minutes or until edges look dry and cooked; turn and cook 2 more minutes. Serve immediately.

## Make It Easy:

*The cornbread mix adds a from-scratch taste with the convenience of a mix.*

# Brussels Sprouts

## with Crispy Bacon and Shallots

MAKES 3½ CUPS
HANDS-ON 28 MIN.
TOTAL 28 MIN.

2 center-cut bacon slices, diced
⅓ cup finely chopped shallots
1 Tbsp. butter
1 lb. (5 cups) Brussels sprouts, trimmed, halved, and
     thinly sliced
¼ cup fat-free, lower-sodium chicken broth
1 Tbsp. red wine vinegar
½ tsp. freshly ground black pepper

*1.* Cook bacon in a large nonstick skillet over medium heat 3 minutes, stirring often. Using a slotted spoon, remove bacon, reserving drippings in pan; drain bacon. Add shallots to drippings in pan; sauté 1 to 2 minutes or until lightly browned. Add butter and Brussels sprouts; sauté 3 minutes. Add broth; sauté 2 minutes. Stir in vinegar.

*2.* Remove pan from heat; stir in pepper, and sprinkle with diced bacon.

### Make It Easy:

**Cut the Brussels sprouts into small, thin slices to ensure quick cooking.**

# Buttermilk Cornbread

MAKES 8 SERVINGS
HANDS-ON 5 MIN.
TOTAL 35 MIN.

1¼ cups all-purpose flour
1 cup plus 3 Tbsp. plain white cornmeal
¼ cup sugar
1 Tbsp. baking powder
1 tsp. salt
¼ cup butter, melted
2 large eggs
1 cup buttermilk

1. Preheat oven to 400°. Lightly grease an 8-inch cast-iron skillet, and heat in oven 5 minutes.

2. Meanwhile, whisk together first 5 ingredients in a bowl; whisk in melted butter. Add eggs and buttermilk, whisking just until smooth.

3. Pour batter into hot skillet. Bake at 400° for 30 to 33 minutes or until golden brown.

## Simple Swap:

**Add a little zip to this recipe by tossing in chopped jalapeño.**

# Quick & Easy Desserts

# Chocolate Lava Cakes

MAKES 6 SERVINGS
HANDS-ON 15 MIN.
TOTAL 41 MIN.

1 Tbsp. butter
1 cup butter
8 oz. bittersweet chocolate morsels
4 egg yolks
4 large eggs
2 cups powdered sugar
¾ cup all-purpose flour
Pinch of salt
Garnish: powdered sugar

*1.* Preheat oven to 425°. Grease 6 (6-oz.) ramekins or individual soufflé dishes with 1 Tbsp. butter.

*2.* Microwave 1 cup butter and chocolate morsels in a microwave-safe bowl at HIGH 2 minutes or until chocolate is melted and mixture is smooth, whisking at 1-minute intervals.

*3.* Beat egg yolks and eggs at medium speed with an electric mixer 1 minute. Gradually add chocolate mixture, beating at low speed until well blended.

*4.* Sift together sugar and next 2 ingredients. Gradually whisk sugar mixture into chocolate mixture until well blended. Divide batter among prepared ramekins. Place ramekins in a 15- x 10-inch jelly-roll pan.

*5.* Bake at 425° for 16 minutes or until a thermometer inserted into cakes registers 165°. Remove from oven, and let stand 10 minutes. Run a knife around outer edge of each cake to loosen. Carefully invert cakes onto dessert plates.

Note: We tested with Ghirardelli 60% Cacao Bittersweet Chocolate Baking Chips.

## Simple Swap:

*Add fresh flavor by garnishing the cakes with raspberries rather than powdered sugar.*

**Simple Swap:**

*You can use chopped walnuts in place of the chopped pecans.*

# Dutch Sorghum Cake

MAKES 2 (9-INCH) SQUARE CAKES
HANDS-ON 25 MIN.
TOTAL 1 HOUR, 47 MIN., INCLUDING GLAZE

1 cup sugar
1 cup shortening
1 cup sorghum syrup
3 large eggs
3 cups all-purpose flour
1 tsp. baking soda
1 tsp. baking powder
1 tsp. ground ginger
1 tsp. ground cinnamon
1 cup buttermilk
1 cup raisins
1 cup chopped dates
1 cup chopped pecans, toasted
Coffee Glaze

*1.* Preheat oven to 325°. Beat sugar and shortening at medium speed with an electric mixer until fluffy. Stop mixer, and add sorghum; beat just until blended. Add eggs, 1 at a time, beating just until blended after each addition.

*2.* Combine flour and next 4 ingredients; gradually add to sugar mixture alternately with buttermilk, beginning and ending with flour mixture. Beat at low speed just until blended after each addition. Stir in raisins, dates, and pecans. Spoon into 2 greased and floured 9-inch square pans.

*3.* Bake at 325° for 32 to 35 minutes or until a wooden pick inserted in center comes out clean. Cool completely on a wire rack (about 45 minutes). Drizzle each cake with Coffee Glaze.

## COFFEE GLAZE

MAKES ABOUT ⅓ CUP
HANDS-ON 5 MIN.
TOTAL 5 MIN.

1 cup powdered sugar
1½ Tbsp. strong brewed coffee

Whisk together 1 cup powdered sugar and 1½ Tbsp. strong brewed coffee in a small bowl until smooth.

## Pecans

The most iconic ingredient on the Southern dessert table is the pecan.

**LOCATION:** The pecan tree is the only major nut tree native to the United States. During pre-Colonial times, they were typically found in central North America and the river valleys of Mexico. After the Civil War, they began to flourish across the South. Today, Georgia is the country's top producer of pecans.

**GROWING:** Pecan trees need well-drained, deep soils free of salinity.

**VARIETIES:** Believe it or not, there are more than 1,000 varieties of pecans; many are named for Native American tribes, including Cheyenne, Mohawk, Sioux, Choctaw, and Shawnee.

# Strawberry Shortcake

MAKES 6 SERVINGS
HANDS-ON 20 MIN.
TOTAL 2 HOURS, 20 MIN.

2 (16-oz.) containers fresh strawberries, sliced or quartered
1 cup sugar, divided
¼ tsp. almond extract (optional)
1 cup whipping cream
2 Tbsp. sugar
6 frozen biscuits
2 Tbsp. melted butter

*1.* Combine strawberries, ½ cup sugar, and, if desired, almond extract. Cover berry mixture, and let stand 2 hours. Beat whipping cream at medium speed with an electric mixer until foamy; gradually add 2 Tbsp. sugar, beating until soft peaks form. Cover and chill up to 2 hours.

*2.* Brush frozen biscuit tops with melted butter; sprinkle each with ½ tsp. sugar. Bake biscuits according to package directions.

*3.* Split biscuits in half horizontally. Spoon about ½ cup berry mixture onto each shortcake bottom; top each with a rounded tablespoon of chilled whipped cream and a shortcake top. Serve with remaining whipped cream.

## Make It Easy:

*Substitute thawed frozen whipped topping for the whipping cream. You'll need 1½ cups of the topping.*

# Mocha Pudding Cake

MAKES 6 TO 8 SERVINGS
HANDS-ON 15 MIN.
TOTAL 40 MIN.

1 cup all-purpose flour
1½ tsp. baking powder
¼ tsp. salt
1 cup sugar, divided
6 Tbsp. unsweetened cocoa, divided
½ cup milk
3 Tbsp. canola oil
1 tsp. vanilla extract
½ cup semisweet chocolate mini morsels
1 cup strong brewed coffee

1. Preheat oven to 350°. Combine first 3 ingredients, ⅔ cup sugar, and 4 tablespoons cocoa in a large bowl. Stir together milk, canola oil, and vanilla; add to dry ingredients, stirring just until blended.

2. Spread batter into a lightly greased 8-inch square pan.

3. Combine chocolate morsels, remaining ⅓ cup sugar, and remaining 2 tablespoons cocoa. Sprinkle over batter.

4. Bring coffee to a boil in a small saucepan; pour boiling coffee over batter. (Do not stir.)

5. Bake at 350° for 25 to 30 minutes or until cake springs back when lightly pressed in center. Serve warm with ice cream, if desired.

## Kitchen Note:

*If you're a fan of nuts, consider adding some toasted pecans. You can also serve this with a scoop of vanilla ice cream.*

**Make It Easy:**

*Make this pound cake ahead and store it in the freezer to pull out anytime you need a luscious weeknight treat.*

# Two-Step Pound Cake

MAKES 10 TO 12 SERVINGS
HANDS ON 15 MIN.
TOTAL 2 HOURS., 55 MIN.

4 cups all-purpose flour
3 cups sugar
2 cups butter, softened
¾ cup milk
6 large eggs
2 tsp. vanilla extract

1. Preheat oven to 325°. Place flour, sugar, butter, milk, eggs, and vanilla (in that order) in 4-qt. bowl of a heavy-duty electric stand mixer. Beat at low speed 1 minute, stopping to scrape down sides. Beat at medium speed 2 minutes.

2. Pour into a greased and floured 10-inch (16-cup) tube pan, and smooth. Bake at 325° for 1 hour and 30 minutes or until a long wooden pick inserted in center comes out clean. Cool in pan on a wire rack 10 minutes. Remove from pan to wire rack, and cool completely (about 1 hour).

## Mighty Mixer

A heavy-duty stand mixer can be a Southern cook's best friend.

**ATTACHMENTS:** This gem comes equipped with a basic set of attachments: wire whisk, dough hook, and paddle. The dough hook makes quick work of kneading yeast breads. The wire whisk attachment is terrific for whipping egg whites or cream. The flat paddle attachment is used for general mixing, including beating together butter and sugar and mixing cake batter and cookie dough.

**BOWLS:** In general, the bowls are large, so they can handle hefty amounts of batter. You want to be sure the mixing bowl has a 4½-quart capacity.

**BUYING:** Before you purchase a heavy-duty mixer, make sure you have the counter space for it. Also, be sure to buy a model that has at least five speeds.

# S'mores-Fudge Pie

MAKES 10 TO 12 SERVINGS
HANDS-ON 20 MIN.
TOTAL 1 HOUR, 55 MIN., INCLUDING FROSTING

2 cups graham cracker crumbs
½ cup butter, melted
2¼ cups sugar, divided
1½ cups coarsely chopped pecans,
    toasted and divided
1 (4-oz.) semisweet chocolate baking bar, chopped
1 cup butter
1½ cups all-purpose flour
½ cup unsweetened cocoa
4 large eggs
1 tsp. vanilla extract
¾ tsp. salt
3 cups regular marshmallows, halved horizontally
2 cups miniature marshmallows
Chocolate Frosting

1. Preheat oven to 350°. Stir together first 2 ingredients and ¼ cup sugar; press on bottom and 2 inches up sides of a shiny 9-inch springform pan. Sprinkle ¾ cup pecans over crust.

2. Microwave chopped chocolate and 1 cup butter in a large microwave-safe glass bowl at HIGH 1 minute or until melted and smooth, stirring chocolate mixture at 30-second intervals.

3. Whisk flour, next 4 ingredients, and remaining 2 cups sugar into chocolate mixture, whisking until blended. Pour batter into prepared crust.

4. Bake at 350° for 1 hour to 1 hour and 15 minutes or until a wooden pick inserted in center comes out with a few moist crumbs. Remove from oven, and cool in pan on a wire rack for 20 minutes.

5. Preheat broiler with oven rack on lowest level from heat. Place pie (in pan) on a jelly-roll pan. Toss together regular and miniature marshmallows; mound on pie, leaving a ½-inch border around edge. Broil 30 seconds to 1 minute or until marshmallows are golden brown. Remove from oven, and immediately remove sides of pan. Cool on a wire rack 10 minutes.

6. Meanwhile, prepare Chocolate Frosting. Drizzle over marshmallows; sprinkle with remaining ¾ cup pecans.

**CHOCOLATE FROSTING**
MAKES ABOUT 2¼ CUPS
HANDS-ON 5 MIN.
TOTAL 5 MIN.

¼ cup butter
3 Tbsp. unsweetened cocoa
3 Tbsp. milk
2 cups powdered sugar
½ tsp. vanilla extract

Cook ¼ cup butter, 3 Tbsp. unsweetened cocoa, and 3 Tbsp. milk in a saucepan over medium heat, whisking constantly, 4 minutes or until slightly thickened; remove from heat. Whisk in 2 cups powdered sugar and ½ tsp. vanilla extract until smooth.

**Make It Easy:**

*Purchase packaged graham cracker crumbs rather than crushing your own.*

# Lemonade Pie

MAKES 8 SERVINGS
HANDS-ON 10 MIN.
TOTAL 4 HOURS, 10 MIN.

2 (5-oz.) cans evaporated milk
2 (3.4-oz.) packages lemon instant pudding mix
2 (8-oz.) packages cream cheese, softened
2 (3-oz.) packages cream cheese, softened
1 (12-oz.) can frozen lemonade concentrate,
    partially thawed
1 (9-inch) ready-made graham cracker piecrust
Garnishes: whipped cream, fresh mint sprigs,
    lemon slices

*1.* Whisk together evaporated milk and pudding mix in a bowl, whisking 2 minutes or until thickened.

*2.* Beat cream cheeses at medium speed with an electric mixer, using whisk attachment, until fluffy. Add lemonade concentrate, beating until blended; add pudding mixture, and beat until blended.

*3.* Pour into crust; freeze 4 hours or until firm.

## Kitchen Note:

*For a homemade look, freeze crust for 5 minutes, and then slip it into your favorite pie plate before adding filling.*

# Skillet Apple Pie

MAKES: 8 TO 10 SERVINGS
HANDS-ON 20 MIN.
TOTAL 1 HOUR, 50 MIN.

2 lb. Granny Smith apples
2 lb. Braeburn apples
1 tsp. ground cinnamon
¾ cup granulated sugar
½ cup butter
1 cup firmly packed light brown sugar
1 (14.1-oz.) package refrigerated piecrusts
1 egg white
2 Tbsp. granulated sugar

*1.* Preheat oven to 350°. Peel apples, and cut into ½-inch-thick wedges. Toss apples with cinnamon and ¾ cup granulated sugar.

*2.* Melt butter in a 10-inch cast-iron skillet over medium heat; add brown sugar, and cook, stirring constantly, 1 to 2 minutes or until sugar dissolves. Remove from heat, and place 1 piecrust in skillet over brown sugar mixture. Spoon apple mixture over piecrust, and top with remaining piecrust. Whisk egg white until foamy. Brush top of piecrust with egg white; sprinkle with 2 Tbsp. granulated sugar. Cut 4 or 5 slits in top for steam to escape.

*3.* Bake at 350° for 1 hour to 1 hour and 10 minutes or until golden brown and bubbly, shielding with aluminum foil during last 10 minutes to prevent excessive browning, if necessary. Cool on a wire rack 30 minutes before serving.

## Kitchen Note:

**Serve this pie with whipped cream or vanilla ice cream.**

# Apple Brown Betty

MAKES 6 SERVINGS
HANDS-ON 15 MIN.
TOTAL 1 HOUR

4 cups soft, fresh breadcrumbs
⅓ cup butter, melted
1 cup firmly packed brown sugar
1 Tbsp. ground cinnamon
4 large Granny Smith apples, peeled and cut into
    ¼-inch-thick slices
1 cup apple cider

1. Preheat oven to 350°. Stir together breadcrumbs and butter.

2. Stir together brown sugar and cinnamon. Place half of the apple slices in a lightly greased 8-inch square baking dish; sprinkle apples with half of brown sugar mixture and half of breadcrumb mixture. Repeat procedure with remaining apples, brown sugar mixture, and breadcrumb mixture. Pour apple cider over top.

3. Bake at 350° for 45 to 55 minutes or until browned.

## Make It Easy:

Tear bread slices into small pieces and process them in a food processor to quickly make the breadcrumbs.

# Mini Berry Cobblers

MAKES 12 SERVINGS
HANDS-ON 25 MIN.
TOTAL 1 HOUR

18 oz. mixed fresh berries (4 cups)
¼ cup sugar
2 Tbsp. butter, melted
1 Tbsp. cornstarch
1½ cups all-purpose flour
⅓ cup sugar
3 Tbsp. minced crystallized ginger
2 tsp. baking powder
½ tsp. salt
⅔ cup cold butter, cubed
½ cup buttermilk
Garnish: fresh mint sprigs

1. Preheat oven to 400°. Toss together first 4 ingredients in a medium bowl.

2. Whisk together flour and next 4 ingredients in a large bowl. Cut cold butter into flour mixture with a pastry blender until crumbly. Add buttermilk, stirring just until dry ingredients are moistened. Turn dough out onto a lightly floured surface, and knead 3 to 4 times. Pat into a 6- x 4-inch (1-inch-thick) rectangle. Cut into 6 squares; cut squares diagonally into 12 triangles.

3. Arrange 12 (3½-inch) lightly greased miniature cast-iron skillets on an aluminum foil-lined baking sheet. Divide berry mixture among skillets. Place 1 dough triangle over berry mixture in each skillet.

4. Bake at 400° for 20 to 24 minutes or until fruit bubbles and crust is golden brown. Cool 15 minutes before serving. Serve warm or at room temperature.

## Simple Swap:

*You can use frozen berries in this recipe if fresh are unavailable.*

# Banana Bread Cobbler

MAKES 8 SERVINGS
HANDS-ON 15 MIN.
TOTAL TIME 1 HR., 5 MIN. (INCLUDING STREUSEL)

1 cup self-rising flour
1 cup sugar
1 cup milk
½ cup butter, melted
4 medium-size ripe bananas, sliced
Streusel Topping
Vanilla ice cream

1. Preheat oven to 375°. Whisk together flour and next 2 ingredients just until blended; whisk in melted butter. Pour batter into a lightly greased 11- x 7-inch baking dish. Top with banana slices, and sprinkle with Streusel Topping.

2. Bake at 375° for 40 to 45 minutes or until golden brown and bubbly. Serve with ice cream.

STREUSEL TOPPING:
MAKES 3½ CUPS
HANDS-ON 10 MIN.
TOTAL 10 MIN.

¾ cup firmly packed light brown sugar
½ cup self-rising flour
½ cup butter, softened
1 cup uncooked regular oats
½ cup chopped pecans

Stir together brown sugar, flour, and butter until crumbly, using a fork. Stir in oats and pecans.

## Make It Easy:

**This comforting dessert comes together quickly with ingredients you probably already have in your pantry.**

# Grilled Pineapple
## with Coconut Sorbet

MAKES 4 SERVINGS
HANDS-ON 10 MINUTES
TOTAL 15 MIN.

1 small pineapple, peeled and cored
¼ cup packed dark brown sugar
2 Tbsp. dark rum
Cooking spray
1 cup store-bought coconut sorbet
2 Tbsp. flaked sweetened coconut, toasted

*1.* Preheat grill to high heat.

*2.* Cut pineapple into 8 (½-inch-thick) rings; place in a medium bowl. Combine brown sugar and rum; pour over pineapple. Let stand 5 minutes.

*3.* Place pineapple on grill rack coated with cooking spray. Grill 3 minutes. Turn pineapple over; grill 4 minutes or until caramelized, basting frequently with remaining brown sugar mixture. Place 2 pineapple slices on each of 4 plates; top each with ¼ cup coconut sorbet and 1½ teaspoons toasted coconut. Serve immediately.

## Make It Easy:

**Use pre-sliced pineapple rings instead of slicing your own.**

# Brown Sugar Pears

MAKES 4 SERVINGS

HANDS-ON 15 MIN.

TOTAL 15 MIN.

1 Tbsp. lemon juice
3 Anjou pears, peeled and quartered
3 Tbsp. butter
¼ cup firmly packed brown sugar
1 tsp. vanilla extract
Crème fraîche or vanilla ice cream
Gingersnaps, crumbled

## Make It Easy:

*Cooking the pears in the skillet rather than baking them in the oven makes this recipe come together in a hurry.*

1. Sprinkle lemon juice over pears; toss.

2. Melt 1 tablespoon butter in a large nonstick skillet over medium-high heat. Sauté pears 2 minutes or until browned. Add remaining 2 tablespoons butter and brown sugar to skillet. Reduce heat to medium-low; cook, stirring often, 3 to 4 minutes or until pears are tender. Remove from heat, and stir in vanilla extract.

3. Serve warm pears and syrup with a dollop of crème fraîche or ice cream. Sprinkle with ginger-snap crumbs.

# Banana Pudding

MAKES 3 SERVINGS
HANDS-ON 10 MIN.
TOTAL 10 MIN.

3 small bananas
9 Tbsp. thawed nondairy whipped topping
1 (3.5-oz.) vanilla pudding cup
6 vanilla wafers

1. Cut half of 1 small banana into slices; keep other half in the peel and save for another use. Layer 1 (5-oz.) glass with 1 Tbsp. thawed nondairy whipped topping, one-fourth of banana slices, 1 Tbsp. vanilla pudding, another fourth of banana slices, and 1 vanilla wafer. Repeat. Dollop with 1 Tbsp. thawed nondairy whipped topping.

## Simple Swap:

Use shortbread cookies in place of the vanilla wafers.

# Lemon Pie Ice Cream

MAKES ABOUT 1 QT.
HANDS-ON 20 MIN.
TOTAL 20 MIN., NOT INCLUDING FREEZING

3 to 4 lemons
2 cups half-and-half
1 (14-oz.) can sweetened condensed milk
¾ cup coarsely crushed graham crackers

1. Grate zest from lemons to equal 1 Tbsp. Cut lemons in half; squeeze juice from lemons into a measuring cup to equal ½ cup.

2. Whisk together half-and-half, sweetened condensed milk, and lemon juice. Pour mixture into freezer container of a 1½-qt. electric ice-cream maker, and freeze according to manufacturer's instructions. (Instructions and times may vary.) Stir in graham cracker crumbs and lemon zest; transfer to an airtight container. Freeze 2 hours before serving.

## Make It Easy:

**Crush the graham crackers quickly by using a food processor.**

# Mint Shortbread

MAKES 3 DOZEN
HANDS-ON 10 MIN.
TOTAL 40 MIN.

1 cup butter, softened
¾ cup powdered sugar
½ tsp. mint extract
½ tsp. vanilla extract
2¼ cups all-purpose flour
Powdered sugar

*1.* Preheat oven to 325°. Beat butter and ¾ cup powdered sugar at medium speed with an electric mixer until creamy. Add extracts, beating until blended. Gradually add flour, beating at low speed until blended. Press dough into an ungreased 15- x 10-inch jelly-roll pan.

*2.* Bake at 325° for 20 minutes or until golden. Cool in pan on a wire rack for 10 minutes.

*3.* Cut into squares; sprinkle with powdered sugar. Remove to wire racks to cool completely.

## Simple Swap:

*For a totally different flavor, use almond extract in place of the mint extract in this recipe.*

# Oatmeal Cookies
## with Toffee Bits

MAKES 4 DOZEN
HANDS-ON 15 MIN.
TOTAL 25 MIN.

½ cup butter, softened
½ cup firmly packed brown sugar
2 large eggs
1 tsp. vanilla extract
1½ cups uncooked regular oats
1 cup all-purpose flour
½ tsp. baking soda
¼ tsp. salt
½ cup chopped pecans
1½ cups (8 oz.) toffee bits

1. Preheat oven to 375°. Beat butter at medium speed with an electric mixer 2 to 3 minutes or until creamy. Add sugar, beating well. Add eggs and vanilla, beating until blended.

2. Combine oats and next 3 ingredients; add to butter mixture, beating just until blended. Stir in chopped pecans and toffee bits.

3. Drop dough by heaping tablespoonfuls onto lightly greased baking sheets.

4. Bake at 375° for 10 minutes. Remove to wire racks to cool completely.

## Make It Easy:

*Microwave the butter for 20 to 30 seconds on MEDIUM heat to soften it.*

# Oven-Baked Churros

MAKES 3 DOZEN
HANDS-ON 15 MIN.
TOTAL 30 MIN.

1 (17.3-oz.) package frozen puff pastry sheets, thawed
Parchment paper
¼ cup sugar
1 tsp. ground cinnamon
¼ cup melted butter

1. Preheat oven to 450°. Unfold puff pastry sheets, and cut in half lengthwise. Cut each half crosswise into 1-inch-wide strips. Place strips on a lightly greased parchment paper-lined baking sheet. Bake 10 minutes or until golden brown.

2. Meanwhile, combine sugar and cinnamon. Remove pastry strips from oven, and dip in butter; roll in cinnamon-sugar mixture. Let stand on a wire rack 5 minutes or until dry.

## Make It Easy:

*Using puff pastry sheets and baking rather than frying makes this dessert come together faster.*

# S'more Puffs

MAKES 12 PUFFS
HANDS-ON 5 MIN.
TOTAL 18 MIN.

12 round buttery crackers
12 milk chocolate kisses
6 large marshmallows, cut in half

1. Preheat oven to 350°. Place crackers on a baking sheet. Top each with 1 milk chocolate kiss and 1 marshmallow half, cut side down.

2. Bake 8 minutes or just until marshmallows begin to melt. Let cool on a wire rack 5 minutes.

## Make It Easy:

**Line the baking sheet with aluminum foil or parchment paper for easy cleanup.**

# Best-Ever Brownies

MAKES 2½ DOZEN
HANDS-ON 20 MIN.
TOTAL 3 HOURS., 40 MIN.

1 (8-oz.) package unsweetened chocolate
   baking squares, chopped
1½ cups butter, cut up
4 cups sugar
2 cups all-purpose flour
6 large eggs
1 Tbsp. plus ⅛ tsp. salt
1 Tbsp. vanilla extract
Edible gold leaf (optional)

1. Preheat oven to 350°. Line a 13- x 9-inch pan with aluminum foil, allowing 2 inches to extend over sides; lightly grease foil.

2. Bring 1 inch of water to a simmer in bottom of a double boiler. Place chocolate and butter in top of double boiler. Cook, stirring occasionally, 5 to 6 minutes or until melted. Cool 10 minutes; transfer to a large bowl. Stir in sugar until blended. Stir in flour and next 3 ingredients just until blended. Pour batter into pan.

3. Bake at 350° for 32 to 35 minutes or until set. Cool in pan 30 minutes. Freeze 2 hours; cut into squares or triangles. Press tops with gold leaf, if desired.

## Make It Easy:

**Use a pizza cutter to neatly cut the brownies.**

# Cheesecake Bars

**MAKES 8 SERVINGS**
**HANDS-ON 20 MIN.**
**TOTAL 9 HOURS, 35 MIN.**

## BUTTER CRUST
⅓ cup butter, softened
¼ cup firmly packed dark brown sugar
¼ tsp. salt
¼ tsp. ground mace or nutmeg
1 cup all-purpose flour
Vegetable cooking spray

## LEMON FILLING
1 cup 1% low-fat cottage cheese
1 cup granulated sugar
2 Tbsp. all-purpose flour
1 Tbsp. lemon zest
3½ Tbsp. fresh lemon juice
¼ tsp. baking powder
1 large egg
1 egg white
Garnish: Lemon rind curl

*1.* Preheat oven to 350°. Beat first 4 ingredients at medium speed with an electric mixer until smooth. Add 1 cup flour, beating at low speed until well blended. Press mixture on bottom of an 8-inch square pan coated with cooking spray.

*2.* Bake at 350° for 20 minutes.

*3.* Meanwhile, process cottage cheese in a food processor 1 minute or until smooth, stopping to scrape down sides as needed. Add granulated sugar and next 6 ingredients, and process 30 seconds or until well blended. Pour filling over prepared crust.

*4.* Bake at 350° for 25 minutes or until set. (Edges will be lightly browned.) Cool 30 minutes. Cover and chill 8 hours. Cut into bars.

## Simple Swap:

*Use fresh orange juice and zest instead of lemon for a different flavor profile.*

# Metric Equivalents

The information in the following charts is provided to help cooks outside the United States successfully use the recipes in this book. All equivalents are approximate.

## EQUIVALENTS FOR DIFFERENT TYPES OF INGREDIENTS

| Standard Cup | Fine Powder | Grain | Granular | Liquid Solids | Liquid |
|---|---|---|---|---|---|
| | (ex. flour) | (ex. rice) | (ex. sugar) | (ex. butter) | (ex. milk) |
| 1 | 140 g | 150 g | 190 g | 200 g | 240 ml |
| ¾ | 105 g | 113 g | 143 g | 150 g | 180 ml |
| ⅔ | 93 g | 100 g | 125 g | 133 g | 160 ml |
| ½ | 70 g | 75 g | 95 g | 100 g | 120 ml |
| ⅓ | 47 g | 50 g | 63 g | 67 g | 80 ml |
| ¼ | 35 g | 38 g | 48 g | 50 g | 60 ml |
| ⅛ | 18 g | 19 g | 24 g | 25 g | 30 ml |

## LIQUID INGREDIENTS BY VOLUME

| | | | | | |
|---|---|---|---|---|---|
| ¼ tsp | = | | | | 1 ml |
| ½ tsp | = | | | | 2 ml |
| 1 tsp | = | | | | 5 ml |
| 3 tsp | = | 1 Tbsp = | | ½ fl oz = | 15 ml |
| | | 2 Tbsp = | ⅛ cup = | 1 fl oz = | 30 ml |
| | | 4 Tbsp = | ¼ cup = | 2 fl oz = | 60 ml |
| | | 5⅓ Tbsp = | ⅓ cup = | 3 fl oz = | 80 ml |
| | | 8 Tbsp = | ½ cup = | 4 fl oz = | 120 ml |
| | | 10⅔ Tbsp = | ⅔ cup = | 5 fl oz = | 160 ml |
| | | 12 Tbsp = | ¾ cup = | 6 fl oz = | 180 ml |
| | | 16 Tbsp = | 1 cup = | 8 fl oz = | 240 ml |
| | | 1 pt = | 2 cups = | 16 fl oz = | 480 ml |
| | | 1 qt = | 4 cups = | 32 fl oz = | 960 ml |
| | | | | 33 fl oz = | 1000 ml = 1 l |

## LENGTH

*(To convert inches to centimeters, multiply the number of inches by 2.5.)*

| | | | | |
|---|---|---|---|---|
| 1 in = | | | 2.5 cm | |
| 6 in = | ½ ft = | | 15 cm | |
| 12 in = | 1 ft = | | 30 cm | |
| 36 in = | 3 ft = | 1 yd = | 90 cm | |
| 40 in = | | | 100 cm | = 1 m |

## COOKING/OVEN TEMPERATURES

| | Fahrenheit | Celsius | Gas Mark |
|---|---|---|---|
| Freeze Water | 32° F | 0° C | |
| Room Temperature | 68° F | 20° C | |
| Boil Water | 212° F | 100° C | |
| Bake | 325° F | 160° C | 3 |
| | 350° F | 180° C | 4 |
| | 375° F | 190° C | 5 |
| | 400° F | 200° C | 6 |
| | 425° F | 220° C | 7 |
| | 450° F | 230° C | 8 |
| Broil | | | Grill |

## DRY INGREDIENTS BY WEIGHT

*(To convert ounces to grams, multiply the number of ounces by 30.)*

| | | |
|---|---|---|
| 1 oz = | ¹⁄₁₆ lb = | 30 g |
| 4 oz = | ¼ lb = | 120 g |
| 8 oz = | ½ lb = | 240 g |
| 12 oz = | ¾ lb = | 360 g |
| 16 oz = | 1 lb = | 480 g |

# Index

©2014 by Time Home Entertainment Inc.
135 West 50th Street, New York, NY 10020

ISBN-13: 978-0-8487-0299-1
ISBN-10: 0-8487-0299-9
Library of Congress Control Number: 2013955775

Printed in the United States of America
First Printing 2014

### Oxmoor House

Vice President, Brand Publishing: Laura Sappington
Editorial Director: Leah McLaughlin
Creative Director: Felicity Keane
Senior Brand Manager: Daniel Fagan
Senior Editor: Rebecca Brennan
Managing Editor: Elizabeth Tyler Austin
Assistant Managing Editor: Jeanne de Lathouder

### *Comfort Food Made Easy*

Editor: Susan Ray
Art Director: Christopher Rhoads
Junior Designer: Maribeth Jones
Assistant Test Kitchen Manager:
  Alyson Moreland Haynes
Recipe Developers and Testers: Wendy Ball, R.D.;
  Tamara Goldis, R.D.; Stefanie Maloney; Callie Nash;
  Karen Rankin; Leah Van Deren
Food Stylists: Victoria E. Cox, Margaret Monroe Dickey,
  Catherine Crowell Steele
Photography Director: Jim Bathie
Senior Photographer: Hélène Dujardin
Senior Photo Stylist: Kay E. Clarke
Photo Stylist: Mindi Shapiro Levine
Assistant Photo Stylist: Mary Louise Menendez
Senior Production Managers: Greg A. Amason,
  Sue Chodakiewicz

### Contributors

Project Editor: Melissa Brown
Designer: Cathy Robbins
Compositor: Amy Pinney
Recipe Developers and Testers: Jan Smith
Copy Editors: Julie Bosche, Rhonda Lother
Indexer: Nanette Cardon
Fellows: Ali Carruba, Elizabeth Laseter,
  Madison Taylor Pozzo, Deanna Sakal,
  April Smitherman, Megan Thompson, Tonya West
Food Stylist: Erica Hopper

### *Southern Living*®

Editor: M. Lindsay Bierman
Creative Director: Robert Perino
Managing Editor: Candace Higginbotham
Executive Editors: Hunter Lewis, Jessica S. Thuston
Deputy Food Director: Whitney Wright
Test Kitchen Director: Robby Melvin
Associate Food Editor: Norman King
Test Kitchen Specialist/Food Styling:
  Vanessa McNeil Rocchio
Test Kitchen Professionals: Pam Lolley, Angela Sellers
Recipe Editor: JoAnn Weatherly
Copy Editor: Ashley Leath
Style Director: Heather Chadduck Hillegas
Director of Photography: Jeanne Dozier Clayton
Photographers: Robbie Caponetto, Laurey W. Glenn,
  Melina Hammer, Hector Sanchez
Assistant Photo Editor: Kate Phillips Robertson
Photo Coordinator: Chris Ellenbogen
Senior Photo Stylist: Buffy Hargett
Assistant Photo Stylist: Caroline Murphy Cunningham
Photo Administrative Assistant: Courtney Authement
Editorial Assistant: Pat York

### Time Home Entertainment Inc.

Publisher: Jim Childs
Vice President, Brand & Digital Strategy:
  Steven Sandonato
Executive Director, Marketing Services: Carol Pittard
Executive Director, Retail & Special Sales: Tom Mifsud
Director, Bookazine Development & Marketing:
  Laura Adam
Executive Publishing Director: Joy Butts
Publishing Director: Megan Pearlman
Finance Director: Glenn Buonocore
Associate General Counsel: Helen Wan